NEVER
GIVE UP
Selected Writings

GERRY ADAMS

MERCIER PRESS
IRISH PUBLISHER – IRISH STORY

MERCIER PRESS

Cork

www.mercierpress.ie

© Gerry Adams, 2017

ISBN: 978 1 78117 537 8

10 9 8 7 6 5 4 3 2

A CIP record for this title is available from the British Library

Printed and bound in the EU.

Contents

For Bernie McGuinness
and
in memory of Martin

Réamhrá/Foreword

This book is a compilation of selected pieces I have written since 2009. I have slightly reworked or edited some of them to make them more suitable for this format. They cover many issues. Some are fairly serious. Others are very serious indeed. A few are whimsical. I hope you enjoy them all.

The period covered includes some very turbulent times in my life, including my move from west Belfast to Co. Louth. I was honoured to represent west Belfast as a Member of Parliament (MP) and a Member of the Legislative Assembly (MLA) at Stormont for decades. I will always be grateful to the fine citizens of that outstanding community for choosing me to represent them, especially because the great and the good told them not to.

I am equally grateful to the people of Louth and East Meath, who sent me to join Caoimhghín Ó Caoláin, the first Sinn Féin TD, who took his seat twenty years ago. There were fourteen of us elected in 2011. I am indebted to former TD Arthur Morgan and to a very fine group of councillors and activists, including Olive Sharkey, Declan Murphy, who managed us all, Máire Grogan, who led us, and Stephen McGlade, who managed the enlarged Sinn Féin Oireachtas team. I was delighted to be re-elected in 2016.

This time I was joined in the Dáil by another local Sinn Féin TD, Imelda Munster, and twenty-one other republicans from throughout the state. Our representation was also increased by seven seanadóirí in Seanad Éireann, bringing our Oireachtas total to thirty. In the meantime, our electoral strength has increased in the North and in councils in both states. Sinn Féin also has four Irish MEPs in the European parliament, representing the entire island of Ireland. Their role in opposing Brexit and promoting equality, solidarity and freedom is very significant.

Some of the issues and campaigns I write about are still unresolved at the time of publication, years after I put pen to paper. These include the search for justice and equality for so many in Ireland and throughout the world. Some of these campaigns are decades old. They are still winnable. The secret is to persevere. Convert the opposition. Win them over. Or wear them down. But keep going. Never give up.

This is an especially important element in the continuing struggle for Irish unity. There is now a peaceful way to end partition. That has been hard won. There is an onus, a duty, on those of us who believe in this objective to persuade those who don't that unity is the only feasible alternative to division and the only way to end all the disadvantages associated with this division for the people of the island of Ireland. The unity of Ireland is an entirely legitimate objective. It is also an economic and social imperative. In these days when Brexit challenges the well-being of our island, people are beginning to see that an all-island approach is the only way to offset this dreadfully myopic English policy.

I am grateful to the Belfast Media Group, the *Irish Echo* and other publications, which first printed some of these articles. My thanks also to Richard McAuley (RG), the great, innovative, incorrigible and constant presence in my activism, especially since he accompanied me on the road to Louth, the Dáil and everywhere else. *Go raibh maith agat* RG.

Thanks also to all at Mercier Press, to Colette and our family for putting up with me, and to our friends and comrades for humouring me.

Tá mé fíor buíoch daoibhse go leir.
Le gach dea mhéin,
Gerry Adams
8 June 2017

FRIENDS
AND COMRADES

XOXO
2018

Martin McGuinness –
A Life Well Lived

23 March 2017

On Monday 20 March, just after 9.25 a.m., Bernie McGuinness, Martin's wife, texted me from Altnagelvin Hospital where she had been keeping vigil faithfully during Martin's stay, to say that he 'was just the same'.

Later that afternoon, at 2.20 p.m., she texted to say he was very weak. The doctors had just told her and their clann (family) that his organs were failing. She said no one else knew except the family. Her heart was breaking. A short ten hours later, at 12.30 a.m., Martin McGuinness died. His family were with him, except for his son, Emmett Rua, who was on his way back from the USA. I arrived in the hospital shortly after Martin died. Bernie was gracious, as always. She let me sit on my own with him.

Even if I had stayed there all night it would not have been enough time for me to gather myself, to get my emotions in check, to recall all the adventures and difficulties, the losses and gains, the ups and downs, the setbacks and advances that Martin and I had been through together for almost all of our adult lives. So I sat there alone in the hospital ward with my comrade. He was stretched out, calm, peaceful and still in death. Eventually I had to leave. I whispered a prayer and said my farewell.

Ireland lost a hero. Derry lost a son. Sinn Féin lost a leader and I lost a dear friend and a comrade. But Martin's family has suffered the biggest loss of all. They have lost a loving, caring, dedicated father and grandfather. A brother and an uncle. A husband.

One of the very best things Martin ever did was marry Bernie Canning. One of his very best achievements was the family he and Bernie reared in the Bogside area in the city of Derry. Above all else, Martin loved his family. So our hearts go out to his wife Bernie, to their sons Fiachra and Emmett, their daughters Fionnuala and Gráinne; to Bernie and Martin's grandchildren: Tiarnan, Oisin, Rossa, Ciana, Cara, Dualta and Sadhbh; to his sister Geraldine, who looked after him in bad times, and his brothers Paul, William, Declan, Tom and John; and to all of the wider McGuinness family.

All of us who knew Martin are proud of his achievements, his humanity and his compassion. He was a formidable person. He did extraordinary things in extraordinary times.

He would not be surprised at the commentary from some quarters about him and his life. He would be the first to say that these people are entitled to their opinions, in particular, those who suffered at the hands of the Irish Republican Army (IRA). But let me take issue with those in the editorial rooms or in the political ivory towers who denounce Martin McGuinness as a terrorist. *Mar a dúirt An Piarsach* – as Patrick Pearse said – at the grave of another Fenian, O'Donovan Rossa: 'the fools, the fools, the fools'. Martin cannot answer them back. So let me answer for him.

Martin McGuinness was not a terrorist. Martin McGuinness was a freedom fighter. He was also a political prisoner, a negotiator, a peacemaker and a healer. And while he had a passion for politics, he was not one-dimensional. He had many interests. He was interested in nature. In spirituality. And he was famously, hugely interested in people. He also enjoyed storytelling and he could tell a yarn better than most, including me. In the early weeks of his illness after Christmas I tried to encourage him to write a book, and he was up for that. A book about childhood summers in Donegal, in the Illies, outside Buncrana. About his mother. His memories of his father. His brothers and sister. Schools days and much more. Meeting Bernie. Their courtship. The births of their children. Their grandchildren. But neither of us realised just how terminal his illness was – we knew he was very ill but did not predict this sudden outcome. Unfortunately, he will never write that book. He was a good writer and a decent poet, with a special place in his heart for Seamus Heaney and Patrick Kavanagh.

He loved growing herbs. He thought he was the world's best chess player. He loved cooking, fly fishing and walking, especially around Grianán Fort in Co. Donegal. He enjoyed watching sports of all kinds. Football, hurling, cricket, golf, rugby. Soccer – he was the world's worst soccer player. He once broke his leg playing soccer. He had a plaster from his ankle to his hip and he had to go up and down the stairs on his backside. And then two or three days later he discovered that he had also broken his arm – I could never figure that out. His mother Peggy – God rest her – told me that he tripped over the ball. He was great at telling jokes.

He liked all of these activities. But he especially loved spending time with Bernie and their family. That's what grounded Martin McGuinness.

Martin was a friend to those engaged in the struggle for justice across the globe. And he travelled widely. He promoted the imperative of peacemaking in the Basque country, in Colombia, the Middle East and Iraq. He travelled to South Africa to meet Nelson Mandela and others in the African National Congress (ANC) leadership, as well as in the National Party, to learn from their experiences. The Palestinian ambassador and the ambassador from Cuba attended Martin's funeral along with dignitaries from Ireland, North and South, the USA, Britain and other parts of the globe. Former American President Bill Clinton gave a wonderful eulogy at the funeral mass.

But Martin was also a man who was in many, many ways very

ordinary. He was particularly ordinary in his habits and his personal lifestyle. He wasn't the slightest bit materialistic. Like many other Derry 'wans', Martin grew up in a city in which Catholics were victims of widespread political and economic discrimination. He was born into an Orange state which did not want him or his kind. Poverty was endemic. I remember him telling me that he was surprised to learn that his father, a quiet, modest and church-going man, marched in the civil rights campaign in Derry. The Orange state's violent suppression of that civil rights campaign, such as with the Battle of the Bogside in August 1969 – a confrontation between the Royal Ulster Constabulary (RUC), supported by a unionist mob, against nationalist Bogside residents, leading to three days of intense rioting – propelled Martin into a life less ordinary.

The aftermath of the Battle of the Bogside saw the erection of barricades and the emergence of 'Free Derry', which was made up of the main nationalist estates of the city. From August 1969 until Operation Motorman by the British Army in July 1972, no RUC or British soldiers were able to enter Free Derry. Martin and I first met, forty-five years ago, behind the barricades in Free Derry. We have been friends and comrades ever since. From his time spent on the run, to imprisonment in Mountjoy, in the Curragh, in Portlaoise, in Belfast prison, through his time as the Northern Minister of Education and later Deputy First Minister – alongside Ian Paisley, then Peter Robinson and Arlene Foster – Martin made an unparalleled journey. And reading and watching some of the media reports of his life and death, one could be forgiven for believing that Martin, at some undefined point in his life, had a road to Damascus conversion, that he abandoned his republican principles, that he abandoned his former comrades in the IRA and joined the political establishment. But to suggest this is to miss the truth of his leadership and the essence of his humanity.

There was not a bad Martin McGuinness who went on to become a good Martin McGuinness. There was simply a man, like every other decent man or woman, doing their best in very difficult circumstances. Martin believed in freedom. He believed in equality. He resisted by armed actions those who withheld these rights, and then he helped shape conditions in which it was possible to advocate for these entitlements by unarmed strategies. And throughout it all Martin remained committed to the same ideals that led him to become a republican activist in the first instance.

He believed that the British government's involvement in Ireland and the partition of our island are the root causes of our difficulties and of our divisions. He was absolutely 150 per cent right about that. The British government has no right to be in Ireland, never had any right to be in Ireland and will never have any right whatsoever to be in Ireland.

Along with others of like mind, he understood the importance of building a popular, democratic, radical republican party across this island. He especially realised that negotiations and politics are another form of struggle. In this way he helped chart a new course, a different strategy. Our political objectives, our republican principles, our ideals did not change. On the contrary, they guided us through every twist and turn and will continue to guide us through every twist and turn of this process.

Thanks to Martin we now live in a very different Ireland, an Ireland which has been utterly changed. We live in a society in transition. The future now can be decided by us. It should never be decided for us. Without Martin there would not have been the type of peace process we've had.

Much of the change which we now take for granted – and people sometimes say to me 'the young ones take it for granted' and I say to them 'that's good, that's a good thing' – could not have been achieved without Martin McGuinness.

And in my view the key was in never giving up. That was Martin's mantra. He was also tough, assertive and unmovable when that was needed. He was even dogmatic at times. Wimps don't make good negotiators – neither do so-called 'hard men'. Martin learned the need for flexibility. And his contribution to the evolution of republican thinking was enormous, as was his work in popularising republican ideals.

Over many years there were adventures and craic, and fun and laughs and tears along the way, and both of us realised that advances in struggles require creativity, imagination and a willingness to take the initiative. Martin embraced that challenge. He didn't just talk about change, he delivered change. He once said: 'When change begins, and we have the confidence to embrace it as an opportunity and a friend, and show honest and positive leadership, then so much is possible.'

It was a source of great pride for me following the Good Friday Agreement to nominate Martin as the North's Minister for Education. It was a position he embraced: putting equality and fairness into practice in the Department of Education, by, for example, seeking to end the Eleven Plus – a disreputable exam taken by students in the North at eleven years of age that determined whether a child went to a grammar or secondary or technical school after primary-level education. He sought to improve outcomes for children and to bring about the most radical overhaul of our education system since partition.

In 2007 he became Deputy First Minister and an equal partner to Ian Paisley in government. And they forged a friendship that illustrated to all the progress we have made on the island of Ireland. His reconciliation and his outreach work, and his work on behalf of victims and for peace – in Ireland and internationally – have been widely applauded.

As part of that work, Martin met Queen Elizabeth of England several times. He did so while conscious of the criticism this might provoke. He would be the first to acknowledge that some republicans and nationalists were discommoded at times by his efforts to reach out the hand of friendship. But that is the real test, and if we are to make peace with our unionist neighbours, we have to reach out. The real test of leadership, after all, is to reach out beyond your own base. It is a test that Martin passed every time.

Some unionist leaders were dismayed at the sight of their queen greeting our Martin on 27 June 2012 or on another occasion when she used a *cúpla focal*, a few words in Irish, or bowed her head in salute to the men and women of 1916. These were symbolic gestures but they were important nonetheless.

As Martin pointed out in his letter of resignation on 9 January 2017, when he stepped down as Deputy First Minister in protest at the failure of the Democratic Unionist Party (DUP) to accept the principles of power sharing and their handling of the Renewable Heat Incentive (RHI) crisis:

> The equality, mutual respect and all-Ireland approaches enshrined in the Good Friday Agreement have never been fully embraced by the DUP. Apart from the negative attitude to nationalism and to the Irish identity and culture, there has been a shameful disrespect towards many other sections of our community.

I quote this more in sadness than anger. I try to understand why this is so. That's what Martin did. At the graveside of this good man I appealed to our unionist neighbours:

> Let us learn to like each other, to be friends, to celebrate and enjoy our differences, and to do so – on the basis of common sense, respect and tolerance for each other and everyone else – as equals.

Let me appeal also to nationalists and republicans – do nothing to disrespect our unionist neighbours or anyone else. Yes, stand against bigotry. Stand up for your rights. Stand against sectarianism, but respect our unionist neighbours. Reach out to them. Lead, as Martin led, by example. By little acts of kindness and generosity.

There was a huge attendance at Martin's funeral. Frances Black sang for him. The flautist Matt Molloy played and Christy Moore sang 'The Time has Come to Part'.

Go raibh maith agaibh also to the choir – Cór Chúil Aodha, under the stewardship of Peadar Ó Riada – from Co. Cork, to Martin's granddaughter Cara, who sang beautifully in St Columba's Long Tower Church, and to the three pipers who led the cortege: Stephen McCann and Paddy and Patrick Martin. Patrick also played uilleann pipes at Martin's house as the funeral commenced.

There were friends from across the entire island of Ireland, from England, Scotland and Wales and from Canada, Australia, the Basque country and from the USA. But it was the mass nature of the funeral, the quiet respectful attitude of the mourners, which uplifted everyone. The vast majority would not have known Martin personally. But they wanted to thank him, to show respect, to be there on his last journey. It was evidence of the great love and admiration that many had for Martin.

Why is this so? It's because he was another of those great and remarkable men and women who have stood up for Irish freedom and for what they believed to be right. He believed that a better Ireland, a genuinely new Ireland, is possible. He rejected any suggestion that gender, race, class, skin colour, disability, sexual orientation or religion should exclude citizens from their full rights and entitlements. That is the legacy we must build upon.

Of course, while much progress has been made – not least in

the numerous lives saved in the last twenty years as a consequence of the ending of the armed conflict by all of the major combatant groups – Irish republicans know that a long, long road, with many twists and turns, still lies ahead.

It's all about rights.

Human rights.

Religious rights.

Language rights.

Lesbian, gay, bisexual and transgender (LGBT) rights.

Social and economic rights.

Rights for women.

National rights.

The right to freedom.

These rights can't be left to any single political party. If you want an Acht na Gaeilge – an Irish Language Act which will ensure equality of treatment by the institutions of the state for Irish speakers in the North – get out and campaign for it. Don't sit back, get out and work for it. *Na h'abair é. Dean é.* Don't talk about it, do it.

If you want a Bill of Rights – to legally protect human rights in the North – campaign for that.

If you want marriage equality – mobilise, get on the streets, demand it.

If you want freedom, go out and take your freedom.

Freedom for everyone.

Organise. Mobilise. Unite for your rights. That is the challenge facing us. To build a mass movement for positive change across all thirty-two counties of our island. And for all our people. Facing that challenge, we are the stronger because of Martin. So don't mourn. Celebrate, organise, that's what Martin would want.

He exemplified all that is decent and fair about our republican ideology and our core values of freedom, equality and solidarity.

It is now over to us to take the struggle from where he has left it. Like Bobby Sands, he believed that our revenge should be the laughter of our children. By his example he showed us that it is possible to build peace out of conflict; to build a fairer, better and more equal future and to build unity out of division.

Martin will continue to inspire and to encourage us in the times ahead. *Ar dheis Dé go raibh a anam dílis.* May his soul be on the right hand of God. *Ní bheidh a leithéid ann arís.* His like will not be around again.

I never thought for one moment I would be writing about Martin like this. Or that I would give his oration. Martin was looking forward so much to stepping down from public office in May. Not to stepping back from activism but to stepping back from the rigours of that particular position. That wasn't to be. But his was a life well lived.

Now none of this is any consolation to Bernie and her clann, but we pray that she and they in the time ahead will take comfort from the happy times they enjoyed with Martin. He said Bernie was his rock many times during his illness. 'My Rock of Cashel,' he told me. 'I am lucky to have her.' Bernie was also lucky to have him.

But so were the rest of us. We also loved him. He will be missed by many. But Bernie will miss him more than anyone else. As I said at his graveside:

> Farewell Martin. *Slán a chara, slán go deo.* We thank Martin Mc-Guinness. He was a rebel. Up the rebels. We salute Martin McGuinness. We applaud Martin McGuinness. He was a Republican. Up the Republic.

The Sagart

Clonard Monastery off the Falls Road in Belfast is a place of pilgrimage. They came in their thousands early on 27 November 2013 to say a final goodbye to a good priest, Fr Alec Reid. He was a close friend, a gentle and kind-hearted man, and as courageous and humble a human being as you could ever hope to meet.

Fr Alec Reid died in his sleep in the early hours of Friday, 22 November. I had been with him the previous Thursday and he was in good form. Talkative, funny and enjoying his hospital tea in St Vincent's in Dublin. But his condition deteriorated. I was phoned on Thursday night and told that he only had days. I arranged to travel down on Friday to visit him but shortly after 9 a.m. on Friday morning we got word that he had quietly passed in his sleep.

I was deeply shocked and saddened at his death. For forty years I had known him as a good friend to me and my family, and a selfless and unstinting worker in the search for justice and peace. In the midst of hard times Fr Reid was always there, offering comfort and solidarity and advice. He was one of the good guys. His death is a huge loss to all the people of Ireland, to his fellow priests in the Redemptorist community and to his family, especially his sisters Margaret and Maura, his aunt Ita, his wider family circle and his many friends.

I first met Fr Alec in the cages of Long Kesh, where I was interned, in the mid 1970s. He and Fr Des Wilson visited the prison often, as they were pioneers of peacemaking in those difficult times. Both men were deeply committed to living the gospel message and to making it relevant to the particular circumstances in which they ministered. They developed dialogue with loyalists and facilitated meetings between us and some prominent people from loyalist paramilitary organisations. Both were tenacious peacemakers.

I met him again on Easter Sunday after my release in 1976, when, at my request, he and Fr Des – who thankfully is still with us – intervened to negotiate an end to the inter-republican feuds in Belfast. They succeeded in establishing an arbitration and mediation process between the different republican organisations – including the IRA, the Official IRA and the Irish National Liberation Army (INLA).

Fr Alec had more freedom than most priests because he belonged to an order – the Congregation of the Most Holy Redeemer, popularly known as the Redemptorists – which fully supported the work he was doing. The Redemptorist mission is to 'preach the values and the blessings of the Christian Gospel to people everywhere but particularly to the poor, the marginalised and the downtrodden'.

Born and raised in Co. Tipperary, The Sagart – as he was known by republicans – was ordained in 1957 and appointed to Clonard Monastery several years later. From 1969, and throughout the intervening years of conflict, Fr Reid was constantly involved in a number of special peacemaking ministries. The objective of these was to give comfort and support to the people living at the coalface of the violence, helping prisoners and their families, and promoting understanding and reconciliation between the people of Belfast. He was also chaplain to and worked closely with the Traveller community in Belfast. Another Clonard ministry aim was to foster dialogue and friendship between the separated Christians of Belfast, an enterprise he took especially to heart, working tirelessly to move the conflict off the streets and onto the conference table.

It was Fr Reid who suggested that we meet with Cardinal Ó Fiaich to discuss the worsening situation in Armagh women's prison and the H-Blocks of Long Kesh, where hundreds of republican prisoners were protesting against the efforts of the British state to criminalise them by forcing them to wear a prison uniform. One consequence of this was that the men in Long Kesh wore only a prison blanket. The Sagart persuaded Ó Fiaich to visit the republican political prisoners in Long Kesh in July 1978. Afterwards the cardinal, then Archbishop Ó Fiaich, condemned the conditions under which the prisoners were being held:

> Having spent the whole of Sunday in the prison, I was shocked at the inhuman conditions prevailing in H-Blocks 3, 4 and 5 where over 300 prisoners were incarcerated. One would hardly allow an animal to remain in such conditions, let alone a human being. The nearest approach to it that I have seen was the spectacle of hundreds of homeless people living in sewer pipes in the slums of Calcutta.

The cardinal informed the then British secretary of state, Humphrey Atkins, of these meetings and tried to mediate a resolution of the prison protest. It failed. The British were determined to break the prisoners.

Fr Alec was also a friend of the prisoners and part of the line of communication between them and the British government up to the first hunger strike in 1980. He actively encouraged initiatives in support of the H-Block blanketmen, who were refusing to wear the prison uniform or carry out prison work, and the Armagh women prisoners, who had their own clothes, but were still refusing to do prison work. Both the blanketmen and Armagh women prisoners were also on a no-wash protest as a result of assaults on prisoners going to and from the toilets.

Fr Alec was devastated by the commencement of the first hunger strike. He had lobbied ferociously for an end to the dispute. The stress of trying and failing to get a resolution took its toll and he became seriously ill. I used to visit him in Our Lady of Lourdes Hospital in Drogheda and on one occasion my wife Colette and I found him in a very distressed state as the health of the hunger strikers deteriorated. Paradoxically, while the plight of the prisoners and their families and the on-going conflict continued to wear him down, he took great comfort from the messages of support that the blanketmen smuggled out to him.

Some of his friends arranged to send him to Rome, where the Redemptorist main headquarters is based. He enjoyed Rome; he delighted in wandering through the city and eventually finding his way back to the Redemptorist house at nightfall. On 13 May 1981, eight days after Bobby Sands died on hunger strike, Fr Alec was in St Peter's Square in the Vatican, reflecting on events in Ireland, the hunger strike and how different the Vatican was to Belfast, with its daily bombing attacks and intermittent gun battles. As he tried to get closer to where Pope John Paul II's procession was passing, an armed man dashed forward close to the Sagart and shot the Holy Father. The Sagart, in a state of some understandable shock and concern for the pope's well-being, made the mistake of recounting his experiences to friends back home. It was a story that was to be told and retold with suitable irreverence in typical black Belfast humour for years after that. Only the Sagart, they pointed out – who was recovering after years of difficult and stressful work, during some of the most dangerous years of the Troubles – could find himself at the scene of an attempted assassination of the pope.

It wasn't until July of the following year that the Sagart was allowed to return to Ireland but on condition that he didn't come north. His superiors were afraid that his fragile health could be undermined if he became re-involved in his previous activities. When he eventually did, we resumed our conversations about the conflict, its causes and how it might be ended. It was obvious that dialogue was the necessary first step. In the early 1980s we tried to commence a process of engagement with the Catholic hierarchy, the Social Democratic and Labour Party (SDLP), and the Irish and British governments. All these efforts were rebuffed. The breakthrough came after Fr Reid wrote a letter to John Hume, the then leader of the SDLP, on 19 May 1986. John phoned the monastery the next day and he arrived at Clonard on 21 May.

Towards the end of 1987 it was decided that John and I would begin party-to-party meetings. The Sagart formally wrote to both of us as 'an interested third party', inviting Sinn Féin and the SDLP to 'explore whether there could be agreement on an overall nationalist strategy for justice and peace'. He presented us with a paper entitled 'A Concrete Proposal for an Overall Political Strategy to Establish Justice and Peace in Ireland'. I brought the invitation to the Sinn Féin Ard Chomhairle – i.e. the party's Executive – and it responded positively. Following this, John Hume and I met on Monday 11 January 1988 for several hours. For the first time our meeting was publicised and there was an immediate and generally hostile response from the governments, the other political parties and sections of the media. Jump forward twenty-five years and it is the same sections of the media and in many cases the same journalists who are still busy peddling their anti-Sinn Féin agenda.

Fr Reid never allowed any of it to distract him and was tenacious in his pursuit of peace. He wrote copious letters to political leaders here and in Britain, and engaged in countless meetings with politicians and governments seeking to persuade them to start the process of talking. He saw good in everyone and lived the gospel message. His was the gospel of the streets. He was there during the so-called 'Battle of the Funerals' in 1988, the first in Milltown Cemetery when the mourners were attacked by a lone loyalist during the funerals of the IRA volunteers who had been killed by British forces in Gibraltar. Three people were killed at the cemetery and over sixty were wounded. Several days later, he administered the last rites to the two British soldiers killed at the funeral of one of the victims of the Milltown attack, Caoimhín Mac Brádaigh.

Fr Reid also helped broker talks in May and June 1988 between Sinn Féin and Fianna Fáil, and subsequently between the Irish government and Sinn Féin. In 1999, at my request, he became involved in the on-going efforts to locate the remains of those who had been killed and secretly buried by the IRA and others. After several years it became apparent that our initial hope that all of the remains would be located quickly was naive. He and I discussed this and we put to the governments a proposal advocating the employment of experts in the recovery of remains, along with suggesting the use of high-tech equipment and archaeological methods. Later, in 2005, he was an independent witness, along with Rev. Harold Good, to the IRA putting its arms beyond use. During this time he was also involved in trying to develop a peace process in the Basque country.

Early on 27 November 2013 we brought him to his last resting place in the Redemptorist plot in Milltown Cemetery. Hundreds of his religious colleagues, political and community leaders and the people of west Belfast attended his funeral mass in Clonard.

The Sagart lived a full life. His contribution to peace in Ireland is immeasurable. There would not be a peace process at this time without his diligent doggedness and his refusal to give up. He remained through all these turbulent times a good and simple priest. He was forthright, funny and totally dedicated to upholding the dignity of human beings. He was an active proponent of equality, particularly of a woman's right to equality.

He was also a proud Tipperary man and a hurling enthusiast. His last words to me were 'Up Tipp'.

Go ndeanfaid Dia trocaire ar a n'anam dílis.

Remembering Friends from the Twin Towers

14 September 2011

I have met the Irish everywhere, from Britain to Australia, from all parts of Europe to Canada and the USA, from the Middle East to South Africa. Some have been first generation. Others have been the sons and daughters of previous generations forced from Ireland for economic, social and political reasons. Persecution, sectarianism, repression and hunger all played their part.

Among the seventy-plus million in the Irish diaspora scattered around the globe, many take a deep interest in developments in Ireland. They seek to play a helpful role. Many times this is in small, personal ways. Over recent decades they have positively contributed to the search for peace. This has been especially true of the Irish in America, Canada, Britain and Australia.

Friends of Sinn Féin (FOSF) USA was established in 1995. This organisation raises funds for the party and has done sterling work in that time. Consequently, leading Shinners have travelled to all corners of the USA speaking at breakfast, brunch and dinner fundraisers and at many universities. We have addressed press conferences, met newspaper editorial boards, lobby groups and politicians at local, state and federal level, as well as the various Washington administrations under Clinton, Bush and Obama (and Trump, as of 2017). We have also engaged with local Irish-American communities and briefed them on the ongoing developments in the peace process.

In my travels around the USA, I have met tens of thousands of very good, decent Irish-Americans. Frequently, in the early days of my travels I would be met at airports by Irish-American police officers, who would whizz me around cities, through rush-hour traffic, with lights flashing and sirens blaring. I used to joke that it was a new experience for me – being driven around by police officers who weren't intent on taking me to prison.

In New York the construction industry and the police and fire services are the backbone of the fundraising project for FOSF. Others, including people who work in the financial district, the law, the pub and restaurant business, in community organisations and ordinary working men and women, have also been enormously helpful. A frequent attender at our fundraisers was Fr Mychal Judge, a Franciscan priest who was well known in New York for his work among the homeless and AIDS victims. Mychal was chaplain to New York's firefighters. He was also a close friend of Steven McDonald, a detective in the NYPD who in 1986 was shot by a fifteen-year-old youth and suffered such severe injuries that he was paralysed from the neck down.

In later years Steven embraced the Irish peace process and established his Reconciliation Project when he visited Omagh in 1998 with Fr Judge. Steven visited Ireland, and particularly the North, many times. This included visiting parliament buildings at Stormont to see the changes that their support for the peace process had helped bring about. Steven – along with Mychal – also frequently attended FOSF events in New York.

In 1999 I visited the Mercantile Exchange, the largest commodity futures exchange in the world, which was then in the shadow of the twin towers. A group of FOSF activists – Todd, Fitzy and Tom – arranged for me to see the place and watch the madness of the 'bear pit', where scores of traders, buying and selling commodities, were lined ten or more deep shouting at each other, creating a cacophony of noise and excitement. How they understood what they were buying and selling was beyond me.

These three also organised a very successful fundraiser in the north tower of the World Trade Centre in the Windows on the World restaurant that year. The restaurant was at the top of the tower, on the 107th floor. I remember looking out of the large windows and it was like being in a helicopter hovering high above New York. There was a spectacular panoramic view of New York and New Jersey, of the Hudson River and the Statue of Liberty, and of Ellis Island, through which so many tens of thousands of Irish immigrants had entered the United States. There were about thirty people there that day, enjoying the craic, getting photos taken, talking about Ireland and being captivated by Rita O'Hare, the then director of publicity of Sinn Féin, who had previously been active in the civil rights campaign in the 1960s, was shot and wounded in 1972, and later spent three years in Limerick prison for the possession of explosives.

We also met security men and women, waiters, lift operators and others. They were all warm, decent human beings. Two years later, the twin towers were gone and almost 3,000 people were dead. Among them was Tom (McGinnis), one of the three who had organised our World Trade Centre event. Another to die was Mychal Judge. Hundreds of New York police officers and NYFD personnel died also, along with construction workers, many of whom had Irish roots.

I remember that day. Martin McGuinness and I had been meeting the Taoiseach in government buildings in Dublin. As we left the building, we met US Special Envoy Richard Haas. The first reports were coming in but the details were vague. Mark Costigan, a very good radio journalist, was outside government buildings with the press pack. He had a new hi-tech electronic gadget with a miniature TV. We heard him exclaiming and so we gathered around him to watch images of the planes hitting the Twin Towers. It was like a scene from a film. It was hard to take in that it was real.

Then on the way north we listened on the car radio to *The Irish Times* correspondent Conor O'Clery's eyewitness account of what was happening. It was gripping, shocking and terrifying. I immediately began to ring friends in New York, trying to find out if any of those we knew were among the dead or injured. Like many others, I spent several hours each day for the next several days doing this, as the extent of the devastation and the scale of the deaths became clearer.

Two months later FOSF held its annual fundraising dinner in New York. It was agreed that the monies raised would go to help the families of the construction industry who were killed at the World Trade Centre. It was a small gesture of solidarity from Irish republicans in Ireland and from FOSF USA to our friends in the construction industry who had suffered grievously because of the attacks that autumn day in September 2001.

During that visit, I called to a local fire station. The fire fighters talked with huge pride of their chaplain, Mychal Judge. He had joined them in the inferno that was the Twin Towers – he died attending to them and the dead and injured. The fire fighters had a deep sense of gratitude to him. There was also a deep appreciation for the huge courage and heroism shown by all those who rushed to help others caught up in the attacks in New York and Washington and the passengers of Flight 93 who confronted their hijackers.

11 September 2001 is one of those watershed moments in human history. Its consequences are still with us today in Iraq and Afghanistan and elsewhere. But our thoughts and prayers are still with the innocent who died. I often think back on all this. I also think of the time I visited Arlington Cemetery with Courtney Kennedy, Robert Kennedy's daughter. She brought us

to visit her father and her uncle's graves. Carved on the wall before Robert Kennedy's grave are words he spoke in South Africa in the 1960s – visionary words in the history of that troubled land but words which also speak to those who died trying to help their neighbours in the 9/11 attacks, and to the seventy million Irish people throughout the world who make up our great diaspora and whose help and support we still need as we seek to advance our democratic goals of peace and unity and freedom for Ireland:

It is from numberless diverse acts of courage and belief that human history is shaped. Each time a man stands up for an ideal, or acts to improve the lot of others, or strikes out against injustice, he sends forth a tiny ripple of hope; and crossing each other from a million different centres of energy and daring, those ripples build a current which can sweep down the mightiest walls of oppression and resistance.

Saying Slán to
Nelson Mandela

19 December 2013

I arrived in Pretoria on the Thursday before the funeral of Nelson Mandela. Irish republicans have a long association with the African National Congress (ANC) going back many decades. We supported each other in our struggles and in our respective efforts to achieve peace. Nelson Mandela and others in the ANC leadership were, and are, hugely supportive of the endeavours of Irish republicans. It was right and proper that Sinn Féin should be represented at his funeral, but it was equally important that we participated as comrades from our struggle honouring a comrade for whom we had the greatest admiration and respect.

The day after I arrived – along with Richard McAuley (RG) – the ANC brought us to Union Buildings in the city of Pretoria where Mandela was lying in state. Richard and I had been here before several times, meeting Thabo Mbeki in 1995 when he was deputy president of South Africa and later when Thabo was president. Union Buildings is impressive. It sits on the highest hill in Pretoria, looking down on the city. It is the official seat of government and is where the president's office is located. This month it celebrated its 100th birthday and was declared a national heritage site.

Between the two wings of the building is a 9,000-seat amphitheatre, which is used for national ceremonies. It was here in 1994 that Mandela, also referred to as 'Madiba', was inaugurated as South Africa's first democratically elected president. It was fitting therefore that it was here that a special protective cover was erected, within which his body rested and through which two rivers of citizens passed by on either side for three days. The queues of ordinary South Africans stretched for miles, winding their way down the hill and through the streets of the city. They began arriving at 4 a.m. each morning and waited patiently in burning heat to pay their respects to their leader. One estimate put the number of people who quietly, sombrely and respectfully passed by Madiba during those three days at over 100,000.

We met our ANC comrades at the Oliver Tambo building and were taken directly to the front steps of Union Buildings. We joined in with one of the steadily moving queues of citizens. Fr Barney McAleer, a Tyrone man who has been in South Africa for almost fifty years, accompanied us.

There was one soldier, with rifle pointed down, standing at each corner of the coffin. The only sound to be heard was the shuffling of feet as we all solemnly moved forward. One behind the other we approached his remains. The top of the coffin was open and under a glass cover Madiba could be seen. It was an emotional moment, a deeply sad moment. Many of those passing by were crying quietly to themselves.

It was at this place in 1994, as he took on the mantle of president of a free and democratic South Africa, that Madiba said:

> We understand it still that there is no easy road to freedom. We know it well that none of us acting alone can achieve success. We must therefore act together as a united people, for national reconciliation, for nation building, for the birth of a new world.
>
> Let there be justice for all.
>
> Let there be peace for all.
>
> Let there be work, bread, water and salt for all …
>
> Let freedom reign.

For eight days the South African government was responsible for the state funeral of their former president. But on Saturday 14 December, as they prepared to fly him south to Qunu, Madiba's 'send-off ceremony' from Pretoria was given over to his comrades in the ANC and to the veterans of uMkhonto we Sizwe (Spear of the Nation), or MK, the military arm of the ANC, which Madiba founded on 16 December 1961.

The programme began at 5.30 a.m. Robert McBride, a former MK activist and political prisoner, who has been to Ireland many times, drove us to the South African Air Force Base at Waterkloof. A huge air force hangar had been transformed into an auditorium. Two thousand invited ANC and former MK activists, as well as international guests from liberation and solidarity movements, were present in solidarity with the family, to give an ANC farewell to their former commander and president.

A space was left in front of a stage for the coffin to sit. As we awaited Madiba's arrival, it was an opportunity to mix and reconnect with people we hadn't seen for a while. Occasionally, groups of ANC activists, many of them elderly women dressed in traditional clothes, would toyi-toyi (the traditional dance of defiance against apartheid) their way back and forward across the front of the hall, chanting and singing songs of Madiba and of resistance to apartheid. It was a joyous celebration of the life of their leader, of the man they called 'Tata', which in Xhosa means 'father' and was a term widely used during the ten days of mourning by political and church leaders, political activists, ordinary citizens and by the media. Madiba was a father to them all.

When his remains arrived at 7 a.m., the South African national flag was removed and replaced by the flag of the ANC. Groups of activists – veterans in the main of the ANC and MK – took turns to provide a guard of honour around the coffin. We were greatly honoured when asked to participate in this. Richard and I took our assigned places and stood silently, paying our private respects to a great leader on behalf of Irish republicans everywhere.

After messages of support from the Congress of South African Trade Unions and the South African Communist Party and others, a stirring speech by President Jacob Zuma and much music, song and poetry, the ANC flag was removed, folded and given to the Mandela family. Madiba was then taken from the hall and flown south to Qunu.

A few hours after that we took a flight to East London in the Eastern Cape province. Here we met some of the other 4,000 guests invited to attend the funeral. A convoy of buses left the airport around 1 a.m. on Sunday 15 December for the long journey to Qunu, Mandela's home and the place he chose to be buried. It was impossible to see anything of the countryside as the night was dark and there were few lights along the road except those of our buses.

By the time we eventually climbed down off the bus, the green rolling grasslands of Qunu were coming alive in the early Sunday morning dawn light. As the sun slowly lifted itself above the hills, its light revealed a landscape similar to the west of Ireland. A big blue sky and distant homes scattered across hills. It was here that Madiba was born and grew up and it was to Qunu that he returned. He was home with his clann after nine days of national mourning.

Sunday was the last day of official mourning. It had been ten long days for South Africa and ten long days for a grieving family sharing their husband, father and grandfather with the rest of the world.

Qunu is an isolated part of the Eastern Cape province. For days it had rained and officials were worried that more rain could cause difficulties for the funeral arrangements. But the day and the sky were clear. In fact, it was a hot summer's day when Madiba left his family home for the last time on the journey to the huge marquee that had been erected to hold his funeral ceremony. Walking into this huge space was akin to entering a cathedral. The South African government had succeeded in creating a beautiful space in which Madiba's life could be celebrated. The ceiling was high, the air cool and the colours of the huge lights changed in the course of the ceremony from blue to gold. The centrepiece of the stage was a portrait of Madiba behind ninety-five candles to mark each of his ninety-five years.

On one side musicians provided music and on the other a choir occasionally raised their voices in song and filled the auditorium with vibrancy and emotion. The event was hosted by Cyril Ramaphosa, a South African politician and activist who has close associations with the Irish peace process. Other contributors included the president of Malawi, Joyce Banda, the Tanzanian president, Jakaya Kikwete – who recalled Madiba's first visits there seeking support for training camps for MK – and Kenneth Kaunda, the former president of Zambia. They all spoke movingly of Mandela's contribution to South Africa, to Africa and to the world. They recalled his many qualities and talents. But all stressed the importance of his legacy and the need to live up to the ideals of peace and reconciliation that he exemplified.

The most moving speech of those delivered was by his close friend and fellow Robben Island prisoner, Ahmed Kathrada, who spent twenty-six years in prison. Frail and obviously distressed, Kathrada described how he and Madiba called each other 'Madala' or 'Elder':

Madala, your abundant reserves of love, simplicity, honesty, service, humility, care, courage, foresight, patience, tolerance, equality and justice continually served as a source of enormous strength to many millions of people in South Africa and the world. You symbolise today, and always will, qualities of collective leadership, reconciliation, unity and forgiveness. You strove daily to build a united, non-racial, non-sexist and democratic South Africa.

But at the end his voice broke with emotion as he said:

When Walter [Sisulu – a former deputy president of the ANC] died, I lost a father and now I have lost a brother. My life is in a void and I don't know who to turn to.

At the end of the ceremony, Madiba's remains were taken outside the marquee and placed on a gun carriage. We were invited to the graveside to watch and mourn as Madiba's remains were placed in the earth, but most of the 4,000 guests stayed and watched the graveside funeral on the huge video screens above the stage. The language might be different and hymns unfamiliar but, as family members placed a flower in the grave and took some dirt to drop in on the coffin, the similarities with our own experience in Ireland were obvious. Madiba's grave is on top of the hillside in which a small garden has been built. It has a magnificent view of Qunu and of the hills where Madiba played as a boy.

When it was over, Richard and I slowly made our way down the hillside to the bus back to East London.

Madiba is gone. But his words are all around us. The legacy of hope and courage and forgiveness and reconciliation is one we must aspire each day to achieve. In our several conversations about the Irish peace process, Madiba understood at once the complexities but also the only direction we could go to avoid decades more of conflict. He supported the peace process in Ireland unequivocally on the basis of equality and inclusivity. He knew that we all had to be part of solving the problems. As he wrote in his autobiography, *Long Walk to Freedom*:

No one is born hating another person because of the colour of his skin, or his background, or his religion. People must learn to hate, and if they can learn to hate, they can be taught to love, for love comes more naturally to the human heart than its opposite.

No Dicket-No Doat

9–13 February 2009 was a really busy week. Monday and Tuesday were spent at Stormont and in the constituency. Wednesday in Kilkenny. Thursday in Kerry. Friday in Limerick. And Saturday in Dublin. It would take too long to tell you all the twists and turns of the road as we voyaged from event to event. Suffice it to say that everyone we met was angry at the daily revelations of chicanery and corruption in our financial institutions. The government, deservedly, is getting it in the neck for the way it is handling this particular can of worms. But that's a story for another day.

When I was in Kilkenny the good people of that fine city in that fine county presented me with a Kilkenny jersey. Gaels will know immediately that Kilkenny were the 2008 All-Ireland hurling champions of the world. THREE IN A ROW, as my hosts reminded me. I was there in Croke Park in September 2008 when they did the treble – outclassing Waterford on a scoreline of 3–30 to 1–13 – and I must say I felt extremely privileged to have witnessed that masterclass in hurling. So I am delighted to have the geansaí.

I was also in Casement Park in Belfast in October 1992 when Antrim beat Kilkenny in the first round of the National Hurling League. Wee Gerry McKeown was there that day also, in another part of the stadium. Gerry was an old friend of mine. A few months earlier he had come to public attention when *The Gerry Anderson Show* on BBC Radio Ulster got a call from a listener asking about the cloakroom attendant who used to work a few decades or so before at a Belfast dance hall, The Astor. He was a funny wee man with a lisp. We called him 'No Dicket-No Doat'. That's what he told everyone rushing at the end of the night to get their coats from the cloakroom. 'No dicket, no doat,' he would shout. He caused pandemonium for anyone who was waiting to leave a girl home.

That call triggered a week or so of similar reminiscences from male and female callers. Apparently No Dicket-No Doat's refusal to hand over items of apparel caused marriages or near marriages, as well as miraculous escapes from marriages and near marriages. The listening public were regaled with tales of romantic liaisons and of No Dicket-No Doat's role in these affairs.

Women rang in to tell how his refusal to hand over a coat led to them being left home by a different beau, and of how they are still married with fifteen children and thirty-seven grandchildren.

'And it's all down to No Dicket-No Doat.'

No Dicket-No Doat, by the way, was a confirmed bachelor and would no doubt have denied any extramarital involvement in the conception of any of these offspring.

'I dread what would have happened if I had married the girl I was supposed to leave home' was the daily refrain of the numerous Romeos who phoned *The Gerry Anderson Show*. Ditto for the Juliets. 'When I think now of how I might have landed up if the other fellah had left me home I just thank God for No Dicket-No Doat.'

So the cry went up. 'Where is No Dicket-No Doat? Is he living or dead?' Eventually wee Gerry was outed as the by-now legendary figure, the cloakroom attendant, maker of marriages, matchmaker par excellence, the famous No Dicket-No Doat and, as Andy Warhol's expression attests, he had his fifteen minutes of fame.

Which brings me back to the Kilkenny jersey and Antrim's

victory against that illustrious county team in 1992. Towards the end of the game, Antrim were in the lead when I got word that wee Gerry was very sick and that he had been taken to a changing room.

I went there immediately and found him stretched out on a physio table while Dr Pearse Donnelly tried to revive him. It was futile. Wee Gerry had suffered a huge heart attack and despite the good doctor's valiant efforts, he died below the stand of Casement Park in the company of a few good friends. Minutes later the ref blew the final whistle and Antrim celebrated a famous victory. The Cats were defeated. But so was wee Gerry.

The next day was the beginning of another really busy week; I was on my way to Derry. It was a really beautiful morning. As was my wont I was listening to *The Gerry Anderson Show*. As our car sped across the Glenshane Pass he told his listeners that he had just received word of the death of No Dicket-No Doat. He then dedicated Sharon Shannon's 'The Blackbird' to his memory. I thought that was nice. Wee Gerry would have been delighted. For a man with a lisp he had a wonderful singing voice.

At his funeral later that week, some smart alecs connected the two events, Antrim's victory and wee Gerry's death. 'It was the shock of us winning. His heart couldn't stand the shock.'

I didn't tell my friends in Kilkenny any of this, or of how the presentation of their county jersey brought back these memories. Instead I told them that Antrim is the sleeping giant of Gaelic games and that our hurlers will see them off again ... some day.

Remembering Fidel

1 December 2016

Revolutionary Square in Havana was packed to overflowing with hundreds of thousands of people. Men, women and children were there on Tuesday afternoon, 29 November 2016 to pay their respects to 'El Comandante' – Fidel Castro. Many were visibly upset – grieving that the father of the revolution and the founder of their state had died. This deep sense of loss and mourning had been obvious from the moment Eric Scanlon and I arrived in Cuba. Eric works for Sinn Féin's international department and for our Dáil spokesperson Sean Crowe TD on international issues.

When we landed in Havana airport on Monday night it was hyper busy coping with the large number of Cuban nationals returning home and foreign dignitaries arriving to participate in the funeral. Among the estimated million in Revolutionary Square there was a sizeable delegation of 3,000 foreign guests. They were there to pay their respects to the memory of a revolutionary hero, one of the great leaders of the twentieth century. And among them were Eric and I, two Sinn Féin reps from Ireland.

Early on Tuesday we joined a lengthy queue of people silently making its way slowly up through Revolutionary Square to the spectacular José Martí monument that dominates it. Many a time over the years, people filled the square to capacity to hear Fidel speak about the revolution and the challenges facing Cuba. Now they were demonstrating their solidarity with their leader in death. On our way up to the monument we met many more making their way back. Most were Cuban citizens – working people – some with their children clasping their hands. Others were foreign visitors on a pilgrimage of remembrance.

The atmosphere wasn't unlike that in South Africa following the death of Nelson Mandela – but was without the toyi-toyi.

Some people we spoke to expressed their concern about the rapprochement between Cuba and the USA in the aftermath of the election of President-Elect Trump. But for me this journey was about Irish republicans expressing gratitude for the solidarity and support Fidel Castro gave to the Irish republican cause. Those who criticise him from within the Irish establishment need to be mindful that he did more advocacy work for Irish unity than any taoiseach. And he spoke more eloquently and more often than any Irish government on the struggle of the men and women political prisoners in Armagh women's prison and in the H-Blocks.

I have been lucky in my life to meet many brave people. Ordinary men and women who, in exceptional times in Ireland or Palestine, in South Africa or Cuba, in the Basque country or Colombia, in Britain and in so many other places, have taken a stand against injustice. In the face of great brutality, they have stood for freedom and independence and an end to inequality and cruelty. Some have been exceptional leaders in the Irish struggle or in other parts of the world. Fidel was one such leader.

In December 2001, along with Gerry Kelly, a former political prisoner, escapee, hunger striker, former Sinn Féin junior minister in the North's Executive and all round good guy, and others, I travelled to Cuba to unveil a memorial to mark the twentieth anniversary of the hunger strikes in the H-Blocks and in Armagh women's prison. The hunger strike memorial is in Parque Victor Hugo – a beautiful park in central Havana named after the author of *Les Misérables*. The ceremony was held on a beautiful, warm winter's day and was afforded full state honours by the Cuban government. That memorial was one of many erected that year to mark the hunger strike. Two months earlier, I had unveiled a monument on Robben Island in the yard where Nelson Mandela and Walter Sisulu were incarcerated for twenty-seven years.

On our first night in Havana we were taken to an outdoor event to mark the formal opening of 200 new schools that the Cuban government had built as part of a programme to expand and modernise its school programme. There were hundreds of people present, including many of the children attending those schools. Fidel Castro was the main speaker and his words were carried live on Cuban television. When it was over he and I met in the midst of the crowd and together we walked about, meeting many of the young people.

The next day we again met with Fidel in his office. We spent several hours discussing Ireland, the issues of human rights, civil and religious liberties in Cuba, democratic values, social justice, equality and other matters of concern to people wherever they live. We also spoke about the state of the world, especially in the aftermath of the attack on the twin towers in New York, which had taken place three months earlier.

It was also an opportunity to thank him for his solidarity with the Irish republican struggle and particularly towards the 1981 hunger strikers. Fidel recalled those events and praised the courage of Bobby Sands and his comrades. He reminded us that in September 1981 he opened the sixty-eighth conference of the Interparliamentary Union in Havana and in his speech praised the courage of the hunger strikers. On that occasion he said:

> Irish patriots are writing one of the most heroic chapters in human history … They have earned the respect and admiration of the world, and likewise they deserve its support. Ten of them have already died in the most moving gesture of sacrifice, selflessness and courage one

could ever imagine … Let tyrants tremble before men who are capable of dying for their ideals, after sixty days on hunger strike!

There is no doubt in my mind that the hunger strikers left a lasting and emotional impression on Fidel.

The revolution in Cuba and the remarkable leadership of Fidel and of Che Guevara inspired many other people around the world in the 1950s and 1960s, and gave hope that change was possible – that freedom and an end to dictatorship could be achieved. Fidel was a freedom fighter whose strategic insights helped overthrow the corrupt and repressive dictatorship of Fulgencio Batista. Batista had a close relationship with American organised crime and when he fled Cuba on 1 January 1959 he is reputed to have taken with him a personal fortune of over $300 million.

Fidel was a political prisoner and a skilful negotiator. Fidel was also a peacemaker – a commitment that his brother and successor Raul Castro and the Cuban government has maintained, as evidenced in their central role in brokering a peace agreement between the Colombian government and FARC.

Fidel was a friend to those engaged in the struggle for justice across the world. Today they and millions more are remembering and celebrating the life of a great statesman who made the world a better place.

In our conversations he was funny, relaxed and knowledgeable of world affairs and of events in the Irish peace process. He was as committed to the principles of the Cuban revolution sixty years later as he had been in the 1950s. He was self-effacing in his humour, totally relaxed and very focused. He asked us many questions about Ireland, including some on our fishing and farming industries. He also asked about unionism. He wanted to hear the sound of the Irish language so he asked that I recite the Hail Mary in Irish while he recited it in Spanish. He also said that following the 11 September attacks in the United States that no progressive struggle would be won by armed actions. They could only be won by the power of ideas and the mobilisation of people.

Despite the difficulties imposed by the US embargo, Cuba, under the leadership of Fidel Castro witnessed economic growth, the creation of a more egalitarian society, and education and health systems which are the envy of many. Under Fidel Castro, Cuba's internationalist commitments saw thousands of Cuban health workers travel across the world providing healthcare to millions.

Like the death of his good friend, Madiba, the loss of Fidel Castro was a huge blow to the people of Cuba and to the world. I travelled to Cuba to extend my condolences and the solidarity of Irish republicans everywhere.

Go well, rest in peace Fidel.

Ar dheis dé go raibh a anam dílis.

Message in a Book

4 September 2009

One of my doomed efforts to escape from internment in Long Kesh on Christmas Eve 1973 led to some of my comrades and I being charged with attempting to escape. There were four of us on this occasion – myself, Big Mick, Toddler and Marty – and we ended up in court before Diplock Judge Kelly. We had, among other things, the distinction of being on remand, interned and soon to be sentenced prisoners all at the one time.

I decided – as we sat in the dock at Belfast Court House and as Mr Kelly was telling us what bad people we were for daring to try to escape from an internment camp in which we were being held without charge or trial or due process – to write a little note to another old comrade, Dickie Glen, who was interned at the time. I had a book which I was going to give him as a going away present and I scribbled in the flyleaf:

> Dickie, I don't know what the date is but Toddler, Mick and Martin are to my right, the judge is to my front and I am on my behind. He is about to give us three years each and he looks very serious. I don't think he likes me writing like this while he is summing up. Yahoo, only eighteen months each. Yahoo, Yahoo!! Toddler is crying his eyes out, Mick is thanking the judge. Martin's staunch. It's time to go again back thru the Crum. Be good. Me.

And then it was back through the tunnel between Crumlin Road courthouse and on to Long Kesh where I found myself in Cage 11 along with Marshall, Toddler and other sentenced republican prisoners. The book was given to another prisoner to give to Dickie. I don't know if Dickie ever got it and he, being in his dotage, can't recall either. The book was Peter McInerney's biography of Peadar O'Donnell, *Irish Social Rebel*.

But the story doesn't end there.

Recently, I received from Louise Ferguson – wife of the late Mickey Ferguson MLA – a photocopy of the inside cover of the book and the message I scribbled in late 1974.

Where was it all of these years? How did she get it? The intrepid RG set out to investigate.

It turns out that Patricia O'Doherty, a friend of Mickey Ferguson's, had the book in her home in Carrickmacross in Co. Monaghan. Patricia's husband, Cahir, and Mickey had both been in the sentenced cages in the 1970s. Patricia was regularly asked, like many other relatives, to bring books and magazines up on visits for the prisoners. Previously on a visit an overzealous and arrogant screw (prison officer) had challenged her after he discovered that one of the books she was sending in was a library book. She was taken into a side office and shouted at, at some length, by this guardian of our library system. Subsequently, Patricia carefully checked books to avoid repeating that experience.

On this occasion when she was taking books in for Mickey, they included the Peadar O'Donnell one with my note. She unfortunately cannot remember how the book came to be in her possession. Occasionally, prisoners would send books out of the prison to their families, or the prisoners brought them from one prison to another when they were being transferred, where they would then be loaned out to other prisoners. So it really could have reached her in any number of ways.

Patricia opened it and read my note. She didn't know who it was for or who had written it and for a time she considered tearing it out and sending the book on into the prison. But she didn't. She put the book to the side.

Patricia meant to show it to Mickey Ferguson when he and Cahir were released, but she never did. But when Mickey died, she showed it to his wife, Louise. They figured out the note was mine and then sent a photocopy of it to me. I gave a belated copy to Dickie, who had patiently waited thirty-five years for a note he never knew had been written to him.

So there you are. Dickie of course, and quite rightly, wanted the book. But he didn't get it. Neither did I.

Ah so …

Máire Drumm

27 October 2016

In the years since her death in 1976, Máire Drumm has become an iconic figure in Irish republicanism. She was an extraordinary, larger-than-life leader, who was a woman, a mother, a grandmother, a political activist and visionary. I heard Máire speak many times at internal party meetings but more often on the streets when taking a stand against injustice. She had the ability to speak from the heart and in language that resonated with people. She was a gifted leader and organiser, and an inspirational public speaker.

Máire McAteer was born in Killeen in south Armagh on 22 October 1919. Her family, and especially her mother, were active during the Tan War and the Civil War. As a teenager growing up in a post-partitioned Ireland, a few hundred metres from the newly imposed border, Máire understood the damaging effect of partition on Ireland and especially the border communities.

She moved to Belfast in 1942, where she began a lifelong association with Gaelic games, serving in senior positions in Ulster and nationally in the Camogie Association. She loved camogie and was one of those instrumental in organising and fundraising for the construction of Casement Park.

Máire also worked in support of republican prisoners and was a regular visitor to them in the 1940s. It was in this way she met Jimmy Drumm, on a visit to Crumlin Road Jail. They were married following his release in 1946. The Drumm family home in Belfast became a centre of Gaelic culture, with Irish classes, dancing and music, as well as discussions on the future of republican politics.

Máire is best remembered for her leadership in the years following the pogrom of August 1969, when nationalist areas of Belfast were attacked by unionist mobs, the RUC and B Specials. Hundreds of homes were destroyed and thousands of men, women and children became refugees in their own city and citizens died.

Following the August pogrom in 1969 the Drumm home also became an open house for refugees. Máire was actively involved in helping to rehouse them. Her daughters cooked for those who stayed with her and she succeeded in getting food and clothes and blankets for many of those who had been left with nothing. It was a time for courage and leadership and Máire Drumm stepped up to the plate. Despite harassment, death threats, imprisonment and a vicious and scurrilous campaign of hate by the British media, whipped up by the Northern Ireland Office (NIO), the British government's colonial office in the North, Máire refused to be bowed or broken, and led from the front. She gave interviews to the media, spoke at public demonstrations and challenged RUC and British soldiers in the course of their raiding of homes.

During those early years of the 'Troubles' the unionist regime at Stormont resisted the demand for civil rights, which were very modest. They were for (in the sexist sloganising of the time) 'one man one vote', an end to the Special Powers Act, an end to structured political and religious discrimination in employment and housing, and an end to the gerrymandering of electoral boundaries that provided for unionist domination of local councils even where there was an overwhelming nationalist majority.

Unionism was opposed to change. It applied the full military and paramilitary resources available to it, including the resources of the British Army. No-go areas existed behind barricades of burned-out cars and demolished buildings. Vicious hand-to-hand fighting and street rioting became the norm. British Army military vehicles such as Whippets and Saracens roamed the streets. Hundreds were arrested – in some instances for simply carrying hurley sticks, and many were beaten. Máire's response to a new law that banned the carrying of hurley sticks was to march to the court with scores of other women, carrying hurley sticks. It was a time of huge turmoil in the life of the state and of families. And it needed an exceptional leader to provide clarity and focus and to give voice to the demands of citizens.

Two of Máire's closest friends and comrades were Mary McGuigan from Ardoyne and Marie Moore from Clonard in west Belfast. They served on the Ard Chomhairle of Sinn Féin together. In 1991 Mary and Marie were interviewed by *An Pho-blacht* about their recollections of Máire. Their memories provide an insight into the strength of character and indomitable spirit of Máire Drumm. Mary McGuigan remembers Máire being ar-rested and going into Armagh women's prison:

> In Armagh she was a great lift to the women. She was much older and to the younger ones she was an inspiration in standing up for their rights. She was also deeply involved in their education and would speak for hours about the conflict and her vision of the future. She was looked on as a sort of mother figure but primarily as a leader.

Marie Moore recalled the curfew of the lower Falls Road in July 1970, when several thousand heavily armed British soldiers sealed off the area and systematically raided and wrecked scores of homes, assaulted residents and killed four men. Máire led the march that broke the curfew:

> We had received word that there were beatings and atrocities happening and no one could get word in or out of the area. Máire along with a few others went around people she knew, knocking on

doors and getting women to organise that first bread march into the lower Falls in an attempt to break the curfew.

There is a famous piece of black and white film footage, which shows hundreds of women marching into the lower Falls and brushing armed British soldiers aside.

Marie Moore believed Máire's focus on demanding equality for women in the struggle and in society was hugely important:

> I remember her saying, 'Look, women were on their streets when their areas were attacked. Their children were on the streets being shot defending their areas. The women were there when the barricades went up. They know all about the political realities of what is happening. They are quite capable of organising themselves and their areas.'

On another occasion, when she was being interviewed on TV, Máire was asked about contraception, which was then an emotive political issue. She said it was something she never had to worry about because the state sorted that out for her. (Her husband Jimmy was imprisoned in the 1940s, 1950s, 1960s and the 1970s.)

Máire was a tireless activist. She was constantly harassed and was arrested many times for her speeches and protests, especially in her opposition to internment. Her leadership qualities and her enormous courage led to her being elected as Sinn Féin's vice president in 1972. I met her many times, including when I was on the run in Belfast. She was always genuinely concerned about how everyone was doing.

Well-known for her defiant speeches at rallies and in courtrooms, she told a judge on one occasion:

> Interning or putting a middle-aged woman in jail will not quench the flame of the Irish people because nothing but the destruction

of the Irish people will ever quench that flame. Long live the IRA! God save Ireland!

Her home in Andersonstown in west Belfast was regularly raided and, following Operation Motorman in July 1972, when the British Army entered the no-go areas in Belfast and Derry, the Brits built a huge military base only a few yards from her home. But she was never cowed or intimidated.

In October 1976, just days before her fifty-seventh birthday, she was in the Mater Hospital for an eye operation. A unionist gunman, clearly acting in collusion with British forces, entered Máire's room and shot and killed her.

I was in Cage 11 in Long Kesh lying on my bunk writing a piece for *Republican News* when the radio reported her death. My first thoughts were of her daughter, young Máire, who was in Armagh women's prison at the time and was almost certainly hearing the news at the same time as I was. And I thought of Jimmy and the clann.

No one from the state ever called to the Drumm family home to tell them what had occurred. Years later a new investigation by the Police Ombudsman began into these events and is still ongoing. But for the Drumm family and for the republican family Máire's loss was incalculable. Forty years later she remains an inspirational figure for today's generation of activists. Her words continue to inspire us as we build Sinn Féin and advance the struggle for Irish unity and independence. In one of her most famous remarks, Máire said: 'We must take no steps backward, our steps must be onward, for if we don't, the martyrs that died for you, for me, for this country will haunt us forever.'

These remarks are as relevant today as they were when Máire said them. We thank her for her life of struggle and we thank all the Drumm family for sharing Máire with us.

Being Donnacha

I remember very well the time my good friend Anne Rynne told me that her son Donnacha had multiple sclerosis. We were on the phone. It must have been about 1995 or thereabouts. Donnacha was in his mid-twenties. Although she was scared, Anne was very brave about this traumatic development in the life of her son. Donnacha was even braver. They are like that, this mother and son, who have faced adversity for every minute of the forty years since first they came into each other's lives.

Donnacha is one of twin boys. Niall and he are the second born of Davoc and Anne's family. Then there is Áine and the wondrous Turlough. Davóg is the oldest. Donnacha's story is incomplete without them, especially his amazing parents. And their stories would be incomplete without Donnacha. He is the touchstone in the lives of his family – and in the lives of many others, including mine. He is a huge inspiration for me.

So who is Donnacha?

Donnacha Rynne was born on 10 June 1970, six weeks pre-maturely. He had cerebral palsy. Anne and Davoc were told he would never walk. Life for him could not be the same as other boys. Not even the same as his twin brother, Niall. There would be no school, no boyish experiences and eventually he would need to be sent off to an institution. Anne and Davoc, however, decided that this was not their way. Their son would be reared the same as any other child. And he was – in the early days in Kildare, and later on the west coast of Clare. He went to school and later to work. For a time he flew the nest and moved back to Kildare to live with his aunt. Following this he moved to Galway, where his mother taught him life skills. Then he returned to Clare.

That's when I first met Donnacha, in the hostel at Spanish Point. My son Gearóid and I were camping our way around Ireland. I knew Donnacha's Aunt Terry and his Uncle Christy (Moore) and I knew of Anne and his Uncle Barry, aka Luka Bloom. That was over twenty years ago. Donnacha was working away at peeling and washing spuds, greeting guests and telling yarns. He was great craic and we hit it off from the get go.

Before long he was in Belfast, up for the Féile. In those days Donnacha didn't need the wheelchair or at least he didn't bring it to Béal Feirste. He was out and about bopping his way from gig to gig, looking for a girl and to his annoyance being chaperoned by a family friend of mine, Minnie Mo (Máire Thompson), who shooed all promising females away. He appeared on Féile Radio and promoted disability rights. He camped in our back room, ate us out of house and home, laughed a lot and charmed my brother-in-law, big Eamon, and especially my wife, Colette, with his take on life, love, lust and the importance of being.

By the time our Gearóid got married to Roísín, Donnacha was wheelchair-bound. But that didn't stop him bopping it up with the rest of us before his father, the ever patient 'sean' (old) Davoc, and his wonderful brother Niall whisked him off again the next day. By now Donnacha was living independently in a house of his own in Miltown Malbay and he and I would get together occasionally for coffee as I wandered through the land. As he became increasingly dependent on carers for everyday necessities, yoga, music and friendship uplifted him.

Now? Now Donnacha has a book. *Being Donnacha.*[1] There are three parts to it: Donnacha's thoughts as captured by his friend,

---

1   *Being Donnacha* is available on the web: www.beingdonnacha.tumblr.com.

Tom Prendergast; sixteen of Donnacha's poems; and short reflections about Donnacha from family and friends.

I am biased. I love Donnacha. Read this book and you also will love him. You will get a sense – but only a sense – of what it must be like being Donnacha, living alone and confined to a wheelchair.

Prepare to be inspired. And his poetry is very good – whimsical and funny. I like the one about his nana:

SCENT OF A ROSE (PHOTOGRAPH WOMAN)
She is getting old and grey we know and her life goes on with love
     of us all,
Some small and hairy faces she hates on all
And put back them shoulders my handsome twin.
Love like the scent of a rose
Give her photo of my ginger sister or any other of grandchild beauty
     and on her mantel of millions it will go.
Love like the scent of a rose
My Nana's wisdom wise is a symbol prize to us all.
Love like the scent of a rose.
Nana
Love like the scent of a rose

Tom Prendergast deserves great credit. Donnacha is very private and brutally honest. Tom's interviews and this book provide him with a platform and a means for expressing himself. Many other citizens in his situation will never get that chance. Donnacha is a voice for them. I thank him for that, for his great courage, wisdom and friendship. As he says himself, he lives in the nowness of life. Well done Donnacha. Keep 'er lit!

BREXIT

Remain Vote must be Respected

30 June 2016

The referendum on Brexit is only the second time since the foundation of the northern state that there was a significant cross-community vote on an issue of political importance. The first time was in 1998 when the people of the North – unionists, republicans and nationalists voted for the Good Friday Agreement. And as with the Good Friday Agreement, unionists, republicans and nationalists once again repeated that extraordinary vote in the Brexit referendum when they voted overwhelmingly on 23 June 2016 to remain within the European Union (EU).

The crisis that the Brexit vote in Britain has caused is reverberating across these islands, within the EU and beyond. The divorce proceedings that Brexit has initiated will not be straightforward. There is a huge entanglement of EU law with British law, which has to be separated out, and this includes the North. The EU is inextricably connected with every sector of life in the North, including the economy, farming, tourism, the health service, climate change, infrastructure, community supports and investment, equality and workers' rights law, and much, much more. Untangling this will be a massive undertaking.

It has also emerged that the Assembly may have to give its legislative consent to repealing the European Communities Act 1972, which gives domestic effect to EU law. So the constitutional lawyers and courts are likely to be busy in the time ahead as they try to sort this particular issue out.

In one important respect the outcome of the Brexit referendum is a vindication of Sinn Féin's long-standing criticism of the democratic deficit at the heart of the EU, of the two-tier nature of its structures and the social and economic inequalities that are part of it. In 1972 Sinn Féin and other progressives campaigned against membership of the then European Economic Community (EEC). Over the decades since then, we have modified our position to one of critical engagement. Our Ard-Fheis formally adopted this position in 1999. We said then that we were keenly aware of the dangers for Ireland as more and more decisions were ceded to unaccountable structures in the EU. So, we also set out our objectives: the reform and restructuring of the EU; the decentralising of power; the promotion of state democracy and economic and social justice; and the creation of a thirty-two county political and economic identity within the EU.

Reform of the EU has been necessary for decades now. The unaccountable nature of much of the EU bureaucracy, and a decision-making process that is often distant from citizens, was part of the reason for the Brexit vote. The treatment of Greece and the imposition of austerity policies on that state and others, also led to anger and frustration towards the EU institutions.

The current crisis, therefore, presents an opportunity to advance the reform project – to transform the EU into something better. Irish republicans want a different kind of EU – a union that is democratically accountable and transparent, and responds to the needs and desires of its citizens; a social EU; a union of equals, of partnership and solidarity, in which member states, at times of adversity, work together in the spirit of co-operation.

It also presents an historic opportunity to end the injustice of partition and to build a new Ireland. The British government has no democratic mandate to represent the views of the people of the North in any future negotiations with the EU. The people have rejected their policy. Citizens in the six counties voted to remain within the EU by a majority of 56 per cent to 44 per cent. The British and the Irish governments must accept that vote. It should be upheld.

Some will say – and I heard this from Fianna Fáil and Fine Gael – that we are bound by a so-called United Kingdom vote. No, we're not. Sinn Féin stands by the vote of the people of the North. We stand for the needs of the Irish nation before those of Britain. That means that the Irish government has to think nationally – not in twenty-six county terms, but for the island of Ireland. It needs an island-wide vision. As a co-equal guarantor of the Good Friday Agreement, the Irish government has a responsibility to defend the agreement and its political institutions. It has to now agree to the maximum co-operation between it and the Northern Executive and to support the right of ministers in the North to deal directly with the EU institutions.

The DUP should also respect the Remain vote. The majority of people, including many unionists, rejected its exit policy. The DUP should accept this – although I'm not holding my breath.

The vote of the Scottish people is what is now determining the political approach of the Scottish government to the EU and to the British government. The Scottish First Minister and her cabinet have decided to put into action their plan to negotiate with the EU and to prepare for a referendum on Scottish independence.

The vote in the North is what will determine Sinn Féin's approach. And it is in this context that Sinn Féin is calling for a referendum on Irish unity. Inevitably all of the usual suspects have lined up to tell us it's the wrong time; it can't be won. The Irish government and Fianna Fáil are quick to talk about respecting the rights of the people of Scotland but not those of citizens on this island.

Irish republicans believe that partition is at the root of the divisions that exist between the people of the North and between the two parts of our island. The Brexit vote has demonstrated that citizens in the North are able to set aside sectarian politics and take decisions based on rational argument. I believe the same can be achieved in any debate on Irish unity.

Moreover, we should not lose sight of the fact that the demographics of the North have also dramatically changed in recent years. The North was created on what was believed to be a permanent two-thirds unionist/British majority. But the last census figures in 2011 revealed that the issue of identity is no longer as fixed as it once was. For the first time statisticians asked about identity – setting to one side the sectarian labels of Catholic and Protestant – and 48 per cent of citizens stated that they had a British only identity or a British/Irish identity. A quarter (25 per cent) stated that they had an Irish only identity and just over a fifth (21 per cent) had a Northern Irish only identity. That means that 46 per cent had some form of Irish only identity. For the first time since partition the unionist majority was less than 50 per cent. Statisticians and politicians are still arguing over the significance of this.

The people of England and Wales have made their decision. They are leaving the EU. If those citizens in the North who voted to remain want to achieve that goal – if they want to stay within the EU – it can only happen in the context of the entire island of Ireland. That's a huge challenge for all of us in the time ahead.

Brexit, Iraq and the Somme

7 July 2016

The end of June and beginning of July 2016 has not been a good time for British politics. The Chilcot Report's damning verdict on the British approach to the war in Iraq and the Brexit referendum result, which will see the British state exit from the EU over the next few years – along with the internal divisions in both of the main political parties – has created a significant political crisis. All of this, but especially Brexit, will have a considerable impact on the island of Ireland, and especially the North. The loss of funding from the various EU sources, including the Peace Programmes and the European Territorial Region (Interreg) Cross-border programmes (which seek to address the economic and social problems which result from the existence of borders), as well as for farming families and the community sector, is expected to be considerable.

Last week I met delegates from the East Border Region programme that covers six local councils – three on each side of the border: Newry, Mourne and Down District Council, Armagh, Banbridge and Craigavon Borough Council, and Ards and North Down Borough Council in the North, and Louth, Monaghan and Meath County Councils in the South. Our focus was on how funding from the EU can be protected following the Brexit vote. The delegates are worried that Brexit puts at risk nineteen projects they are currently developing worth a total of €132 million. They are not alone in this concern.

Theresa May is now the British Prime Minister and has the responsibility for managing the British disengagement from the

EU, but she also has a responsibility in implementing the Good Friday Agreement. In April she publicly announced her commitment to ending the British government's involvement with the European Convention on Human Rights. The Tories have also stated their desire to scrap the Human Rights Act, which, according to the human rights group Liberty, 'would amount to a serious breach of the Good Friday Agreement'. These are the essential rights frameworks within the Good Friday Agreement which are needed to ensure there will be no repeat of the past policies of discrimination and repression that were a part of the northern state from the time of partition.

As co-equal guarantor of the Good Friday Agreement, the Irish government has an onerous responsibility to defend this international treaty and the human rights elements of it. The Taoiseach must make very clear to Prime Minister May that the Irish government will not countenance any action by the British government that will undermine the integrity of the 1998 agreement and subsequent agreements.

However, the fallout from the Chilcot Report continues to reverberate. Chilcot accused Tony Blair of invading Iraq before all 'peaceful options for disarmament had been exhausted. Military action at that time was not a last resort.' Much attention has also focused on the former British Prime Minister's words to George W. Bush eight months before the invasion: 'I will be with you, whatever.' What emerges from Chilcot's two and a half million words is a British government that had not prepared its military for the invasion. It had neither the right military equipment nor the necessary strategies essential to an invasion. Nor did it adequately plan for any political vacuum arising from the defeat of Saddam Hussein. Like David Cameron, who had no plan for a successful 'leave' Brexit vote, Tony Blair had no post-invasion strategy.

In the course of Sinn Féin's negotiations in 2002 with Tony Blair, both Martin McGuinness and I raised the prospect of an Iraq invasion with him. We told Mr Blair and his colleagues very strongly that an invasion would be wrong. We also warned him that, in our view, the outcome of any war would be a disaster for the people of Iraq and the British people. We put this to him in a very forthright way on a number of occasions. It was very clear to us from those conversations, many months before a public decision to invade was announced, that Mr Blair was committed to this course of action.

At the same time as the Chilcot Report was being published, commemorations were being held in France, Britain and here in Ireland in remembrance of the victims of an earlier conflict. The Battle of the Somme began on 1 July 1916 and ended in November of that year. The report of the Chilcot inquiry into the invasion of Iraq is a reminder of how little the British state has learned in the intervening 100 years. The similarities are striking. Disastrous political decisions and the ill-preparedness of the British military in attacking the German lines at the Somme in July 1916 are reflected in the invasion of Iraq in January 2003.

On 1 July 1916, after five days in which over a million shells were fired by the British artillery, British soldiers, including many Irish, went 'over the top' and into no man's land. They did so believing that the barbed wire lines had been destroyed. However, because of poor quality control, a huge percentage of the artillery shells were duds. Most of those that did explode were shrapnel shells, which were largely ineffective against the German soldiers in their deep dugouts and against the barbed-wire entanglements. At the end of that first day, the British Army had lost 60,000 men, a third of them dead and many others who would never fight again. When the battle finally ended in November, 420,000 British Army men, about 200,000 French and around half a million Germans had been killed or injured. No side had won.

Like Iraq eighty-seven years later, and many other post-colonial conflicts after 1945, British military planning was inept, military equipment was often ineffective and the decisions of its political leadership doomed many soldiers and civilians to death. These wars, like those in the North, in Kenya, Yemen, Palestine and Afghanistan and many more, were the result of bad political decisions and the willingness of political leaders to hand over responsibility for political disputes to the generals, which, in all these cases, was a recipe for disaster.

Brexit Battle Lines are Drawn

5 October 2016

After months of confusion over what Brexit will mean in practice the British Prime Minister, Theresa May, has finally given some substance to her 'Brexit means Brexit' line. The Conservative Party conference was an opportunity for the Tory Brexiteers in the British cabinet to finally spell out the direction they plan to take. According to Mrs May the British government will trigger Article 50 before the end of March 2017. This will begin the two-year process of negotiation by the end of which the British state will have left the EU. The British Prime Minister has now set the British state on the path to a so-called 'hard Brexit', that is a new political and economic relationship with the EU in which Britain is outside of the customs union and the Single Market. This will impact enormously on trade arrangements, including the potential for World Trade Organisation tariffs being imposed on goods. In addition, sectors like agri-food and agriculture would have to pay more to export and could lose protections against cheaper imports. Leaving the customs union will also mean a significant increase in customs checks and a longer period of time for the processing of British goods travelling into the EU.

The emphasis in May's speech was on independence and sovereignty, with Britain taking back full control of immigration. Consequently, there will be no free movement of workers as the barriers to immigrants are raised and reinforced. She also said that Britain would leave the European Court of Justice, which is the ultimate enforcer of European laws. As I mentioned before, the Tories are already committed to scrapping the Human Rights Act and leaving the European Court of Human Rights.

By insisting that Britain pursue a 'hard Brexit' Theresa May has set Britain on a collision course with the EU, in which Ireland, North and South, is regarded as collateral damage. She has moved from supporting the 'Remain' side in the referendum last June to kowtowing to the right wing of her own party. In the months since the Brexit vote there has been widespread concern that the North–South border will become an international frontier.

There were those who hoped that Britain would opt for a 'soft' option. The examples of the border between Norway and Sweden and the EU relationship with Switzerland were frequently promoted. In her speech at the Conservative Party conference Mrs May rubbished both. As a result, the British approach now puts in doubt the maintenance of the 'common travel area' between Ireland and Britain, which has existed since 1923. It also raises serious questions about the shape of the border post-Brexit: the free movement of citizens and the likely impact on cross-border and bilateral trade, which accounts for one billion euro a week between Ireland and Britain and which supports 200,000 jobs.

Edgar Morgenroth, an adviser to the Irish government, warned that the British stance 'imperils the Common Travel Area'. He also warned against the belief that Dublin could negotiate some form of bilateral agreement with the British on trade and the movement of people. Under EU rules he pointed out that there are 'no bilaterals here. It's always the twenty-seven EU countries and the UK.'

Prime Minister May called for preparatory work to be carried out between the EU and Britain in advance of March to facilitate a smoother process of negotiation. The response from the EU was immediate and dismissive. Donald Tusk, the president of the European Council, rejected any suggestion of preliminary talks.

The EU commission has also warned Britain that there will be no informal discussions before Article 50 has been triggered. And media reports also suggested that the German chancellor, Angela Merkel, is against informal negotiations.

So, the battle lines on Brexit have been drawn.

The Tories are determined to exit the EU. They are also intent on pulling the North and Scotland out of the EU, despite both having voted overwhelmingly to remain. Mrs May told her party conference that there will be 'no opt-out from Brexit' and so the Remain votes in the North and in Scotland are to be set aside. The parliamentary convention that the Westminster parliament will only legislate on matters affecting either the North or Scotland or Wales with the consent of the local assemblies is also to be ignored.

Martin McGuinness insisted that the Remain vote in the North must be respected in any negotiation. He warned that the British government's confrontational approach to Brexit threatens the North's economy and the Good Friday and subsequent agreements. While both he and Arlene Foster are committed to doing their best for citizens, the reality is that the DUP is committed to Brexit and this makes the political relationships and situation more problematic.

Two legal challenges began in Belfast High Court at the same time. One is being taken by Raymond McCord and the other by a group of MLAs, including Sinn Féin MLA John O'Dowd, SDLP leader Colum Eastwood, Steven Agnew of the Green Party and David Ford, the Alliance leader. Their legal team will contest the legality of the process and they will argue that the North cannot leave the EU without the consent of the assembly.

Also in its response to Brexit the Irish government finally produced a series of proposals, including the establishment of an All-Island Civic Dialogue, bringing together political, community and business leaders from across the island to discuss the implications of Brexit. In July the Taoiseach had promised to bring the all-island dialogue forward in September. He failed to do this, which is why I accused him of dithering on this issue.

The establishment parties of Fine Gael and Fianna Fáil seem to be mesmerised by what the British government is going to do, as opposed to what the Irish government should be doing. Irish national interests have to be protected and promoted.

Addendum

The All-Island Civic Dialogue began its deliberations in Dublin on 2 November 2016. This is a good initiative but only if the government takes it seriously, allows for a real dialogue and acts on the advice it is given. Time will tell.

However, its overriding priority must be to advocate on behalf of the Remain vote in the North. It's worth remembering that 56 per cent of the electorate backed remaining within the EU – a strong majority – and the Irish government must defend this vote. On 28 September 2016, when I raised this with Taoiseach Enda Kenny in the Dáil, as I had done on previous occasions, he said, 'I accept that the result of the vote on Brexit was that the people of Northern Ireland, by majority, voted to stay in the EU. I will articulate this point at the discussions that take place at European Council level.'

Our focus in the time ahead must be to agree an all-island strategy that challenges Brexit. Martin McGuinness said that Brexit is not a done deal. He was right.

Standing up for
Ireland in the EU

10 November 2016

The British political establishment and media like to describe Westminster as the 'mother of parliaments'. They ignore the cruel exploitation of scores of colonies approved by those in Westminster during centuries of empire and the widespread use of violence to suppress democratic demands. All of this is regularly brushed aside as the British system endlessly praises itself and inflates its sense of self-importance. Earlier this year an opinion poll found that 44 per cent of people in Britain were proud of its history of colonialism, while only 21 per cent regretted that it happened. The same poll also asked whether the British Empire was a good thing or a bad thing: 43 per cent said it was good, while only 19 per cent said it was bad. Twenty-five per cent responded that it was 'neither'. I would be confident that a similar poll in any of Britain's colonies would paint a starkly different picture.

The British are especially proud of their judicial system. This is despite the many miscarriages of justice against Irish people it perpetrated during the 1970s and 1980s. However, the recent decision by the British High Court – that Theresa May has to seek parliamentary approval to trigger Article 50 of the Lisbon Treaty to begin the Brexit negotiation – has led to a deepening crisis within the British state. One right-wing British newspaper branded the three judges who took this decision as 'enemies of the people'. The British right-wing politician Nigel Farage has warned of violence on the streets and added to this increasingly fraught atmosphere with a plan to hold a 100,000 strong march in London on the day the British Supreme Court assembles to hear the appeal on 5 December. Does the British government know what it is doing? There is ample evidence to suggest it doesn't. In the meantime, the crisis for the island of Ireland around Brexit deepens with each passing day.

Recently the Irish government held its All-Island Civic Dialogue forum on Brexit in Dublin. While the unionist parties disappointingly refused to attend, nonetheless it was a valuable, wide-ranging conference that heard the views of political parties, economists, the civic and business sectors, the voices of rural Ireland and of agriculture, and of those community organisations that rely on EU funding. Sinn Féin's speakers highlighted the need for political alternatives to Brexit to be agreed upon and for a diplomatic offensive, led by the Irish government, to build support for a designated special status for the North within the EU.

A study published by the Department of Finance in Dublin, and the Economic and Social Research Institute, concluded that Brexit was going to be bad for the Irish state. It found that a hard Brexit would permanently damage the economy, reducing its size by almost 4 per cent and increasing unemployment by as much as 2 per cent.

Martin McGuinness, Michelle O'Neill and I met Taoiseach Enda Kenny and the Irish Minister for Foreign Affairs, Charlie Flanagan, at parliament buildings when they were at Stormont meeting some of the political parties about Brexit. Our conversation with them was part of Sinn Féin's on-going efforts to secure the position of the island of Ireland within the EU, which is crucial given that Brexit will reshape arrangements and relationships between these islands and between the EU and us. Our task must be to ensure that any new arrangements on this island are to the mutual benefit of everyone who lives here. This means there is an obligation on all of us to explore alternatives to Brexit – and all options available to ensure that the North can remain within the EU.

Rather than wait to see what the British government does, we need to be proactive about setting out alternatives – constitutional, political and otherwise – that protect and promote the national interests of our island. Specifically, we believe that there is a need to build support for a designated special status for the North within the EU. This status would threaten no one's constitutional preference, and the Irish government, as a continuing member of the EU, has the right, and in our view the obligation, to bring forward such a proposal.

There is also a particular duty on the Irish government, as a member state of the EU and as co-guarantor of the Good Friday Agreement, to strongly safeguard the political, constitutional and legal integrity of the agreement – an international agreement – in all its parts. British governments have no difficulty acting in their perceived national interests. The Irish government must also act nationally, in the accurate and meaningful sense of that word. It means defending the interests and the rights of the people of this island.

As well as the enormous and unprecedented economic challenges that face us, the entire post-Good Friday Agreement all-island institutional and political architecture is under very serious threat from Brexit. For example:

- The Conservative government has refused to put in place a Bill of Rights agreed in 1998.

- They refuse to legislate for the rights of Irish speakers through an Acht na Gaeilge that was agreed at St Andrews in October 2006.

- The British government is planning to scrap the Human Rights Act and to end their relationship with the European Convention on Human Rights, which are integral parts of the Good Friday Agreement human rights infrastructure.

As we seek to forge strategies to meet this challenge there are obvious priorities. These must include maintaining the Common Travel Area, which allows for the free travel, residence and the right to work and to draw social benefits between the Irish state and Britain. This predates Irish and British membership of the EU and is not dependent on EU membership. There also needs to be a specific focus on EU funding. The North and the southern border counties depend on funding programmes, including Interreg and PEACE, to continue building the peace and developing the economy. The cross-border structural funds bring massive economic and social benefits. The Common Agricultural Payments (CAP) subsidy is essential for farmers.

Finally, there are the implementation bodies that exist because of the Good Friday Agreement. The North/South Ministerial Council manages six All-Ireland implementation bodies working on a cross-border basis, including InterTradeIreland, Waterways, Foras, Irish Lights, SafeFood and the Special EU Programmes Body (SEUPB), which administers the cross-border EU funding. All of these elements, and the specific agreements on health provision and other matters, are part of an interlocking institutional and constitutional arrangement that has maintained the peace for almost twenty years. All of this is now at risk because of Brexit.

There is, therefore, an urgency and an obligation to move the process forward and begin to look at alternatives to Brexit. That means accepting and acting in line with the will of citizens in the North to remain in the EU. The decisions we take and the strategies we pursue will impact on generations to come. The choice is simple – acquiesce to the demands of London and allow the North to be dragged out of the EU, or pursue the credible path to argue at European level and with the British government for the North to be designated a special status within the EU.

Just as there are massive challenges, there is also the opportunity to plot a new course and stand up for the majority of people who voted to remain, to stand up for our national economic interests of all-Ireland trade and employment, and to stand up for the agreements and progress.

An Irish Solution
to an English Problem

11 May 2017

Sinn Féin campaigned against Irish membership of the EEC in 1973. Since then, every European treaty has taken further powers from the Irish state. Sinn Féin wants a different type of EU. We want a social Europe which promotes peace, demilitarisation, economic and social justice, international solidarity and greater democratic accountability.

Today's EU is wedded to neoliberal policies which have created widespread hardship as austerity, deregulation and privatisation have undermined the social function of states and the rights of citizens and workers. This is especially evident in the way the EU elites foisted €65 billion of private banking debt on Irish citizens. The Austerity Treaty imposed excessively rigid rules which limit the ability of governments to invest in infrastructure and public services as part of a counter-cyclical approach to tackling recession and returning to economic growth.

People across the EU are increasingly alienated from the EU. This has assisted the growth of far-right parties which exploit people's fears. Brexit is a consequence of that. Thankfully Ireland is not affected by this growth, except for some elements in the North on the more conservative edges of unionism.

During the Brexit referendum, Sinn Féin campaigned for a Remain vote in the North. It is clearly not in the interests of the people of this island, whatever their background or views, to have one part of the island outside the EU while the other part is inside. The

EU has supported the peace process and the Good Friday Agreement going back to the time of John Hume and David Trimble. The other member states must know that any EU agreement which violates an international treaty, which is what the Good Friday Agreement is, would contravene EU treaty obligations.

Brexit is not only an issue for the North. It will adversely affect the entire island if we let it. It is vital that its challenges are met on an all-island basis. It is already having a serious and detrimental effect on Irish jobs and businesses, in particular in the agriculture and agri-food sectors. The aim of the EU should be to prevent a land frontier between the EU and Britain on the island of Ireland. That should be the key objective and the priority. To achieve this, we have advocated that the North be afforded designated special status within the EU.

Most thoughtful people also believe that Ireland should have a veto on any agreement reached between the EU and the British government that does not include this position. Designated status is the best and only way to ensure that the entire island of Ireland will remain within the EU. It is an imaginative solution that addresses the complexities of the problem. It does not affect the constitutional status of the North. That will be changed only by a referendum.

Designated special status within the EU is the position endorsed by the Dáil. It is supported by the majority of MLAs in the Northern Assembly. It recognises that the people of the North voted to remain part of the EU. It is a solution being advocated by representatives of border communities. Is that just going to be placed to one side, ignored or driven over? The Tory government in England should not be allowed to reject the vote in the North and set aside the decision of people there. It should not be allowed to drive the North out of the EU against the democratic wishes of its citizens.

Designated special status for the North within the EU is not about a hard Brexit or a soft Brexit; it is about the best interests of our economy, our peace process and our people. It is also a democratic imperative. It is about retaining the freedom of movement of goods, people and services on the island of Ireland.

Any restriction whatsoever on freedom of movement would represent a hardening of the border. Believe me, this will severely damage social and economic cohesion. It would also be unacceptable to those who live in border communities and to people right across our island. Special status would ensure the North's trading relationship with the rest of Ireland and the EU, particularly in the context of business, tourism, the all-Ireland energy market, agriculture and the agri-food sector. All the relationships in this regard need to be maintained. It is about allowing all of Ireland to remain in the customs union and the Single Market and under the jurisdiction of the European Court of Justice.

Special status is also about maintaining the European Convention on Human Rights in the North and protecting the rights of citizens who have a right to Irish citizenship and, therefore, to citizenship of the EU. Access to EU rights and services across employment, workers' conditions, social security and healthcare must also be protected.

None of this is beyond our collective wisdom or ability. It will require political flexibility from the EU. Of course, the little Englanders – those who embrace English jingoism – may object. But the reality is that they are looking for special arrangements with the EU for themselves. There are already unique arrangements in place for other states. Therefore, the EU has a history of being flexible on these matters. There are different forms of integration and relationships for member states and non-member states. These include overseas countries and territory status, the European Free Trade Association and the separate customs union.

In light of the provisions for Irish unity in the Good Friday Agreement, the EU should not diverge from these norms. Sinn Féin would like to see a referendum on Irish unity within the next five years. The immediate challenge facing the EU and the people of Ireland now, however, is how to meet the threat of Brexit. This is all about what kind of Ireland will emerge after Brexit. The only way to shape that positively is through designated special status for the North within the EU.

THE IRISH
PEACE PROCESS

British Secretaries of State
I Have Known

27 July 2016

Martin McGuinness told British Prime Minister Theresa May that following the Brexit vote the British government will have to respect the democratically expressed wishes of the people of the North who see their future in the EU and voted to remain there. Time will tell whether or not she commits to this.

As a new leader, Mrs May will undoubtedly have a lot of issues and jobs to tackle in the coming weeks and months. One of her first jobs on becoming Prime Minister on 13 July 2016 was to appoint a new secretary of state for the North. Believe it or not the new occupant of Hillsborough Castle – James Brokenshire – is the nineteenth British politician to hold that position.

The first was William Whitelaw in 1972, who was appointed after the Conservative government of Ted Heath had decided to consign the unionist regime at Stormont to the dustbin of history. In the absence of a government in the North, the secretaries of state essentially ran the place. (Whitelaw was also the first that I met, as republicans attempted to negotiate with the British government in the summer of that year, but that's a story for another time.)

The role has changed over the years. Under the devolved structures established by the Good Friday Agreement the power of the secretary of state is limited to representing the North in the British Cabinet. He or she also has responsibility for overseeing

85

the running of the devolved structures and a number of other matters, including human rights and elections, which are reserved under their control.

Apart from Theresa Villiers and Mo Mowlam, all the secretaries of state were men. Some were friendlier than others. Some of them were downright Machiavellian in their machinations. But all of them were in the North to defend and promote British national interests. These interests rarely coincided with the interests of the people of the North or of the island of Ireland.

They were a mixed bunch in terms of ability. Most were distant and aloof and most were also in the pockets of the generals and securocrats and the intelligence services. I suspect some of them liked to play at being M in James Bond.

Merlyn Rees, who was secretary of state from March 1974 until September 1976, came across as a bit of a bumbler. But it was he who introduced the criminalisation policy and built the H-Blocks. Roy Mason, who replaced Rees and held the post until May 1979, was an arrogant wee man with a Napoleonic complex who believed that he would 'squeeze the IRA like a tube of toothpaste'. Under his watch, torture was routinely used in the interrogation centres in the RUC's Castlereagh centre, Gough Barracks in Armagh, Strand Road in Derry and other places. It was Mason who presided over the 'conveyor belt' system of arrest – torture – Diplock non-jury courts and the H-Blocks and Armagh women's prison. The law became another weapon in the British arsenal to defeat republicans.

After Margaret Thatcher became British Prime Minister in May 1979 she appointed Humphrey Atkins to the position. A local wit painted a graffiti question, 'Humphrey WHO?', on the wall at Beechmount Leisure centre on the Falls Road. Atkins was the secretary of state during one of the most turbulent periods in the 'Troubles'. Under his watch the hunger strikes of 1980 and 1981 occurred. He was the face of Thatcher in the media, defending British inflexibility. Those who followed him during the 1980s were all Thatcher's men. In my memory they all merge into one other.

After Whitelaw in 1972, the first British secretary of state that I met was Patrick Mayhew, who was appointed in April 1992 and was there until April 1997. As British attorney-general, he had agreed a deal in 1992 with Brian Nelson, a British agent within the UDA, which saw charges of murder against Nelson dropped to avoid embarrassing revelations about the role of the British state in collusion. Mayhew was also in the North when the media broke the story of secret contacts for over three years between republicans and the British government. Mayhew initially denied this but, following intense media speculation, he then announced that it was his intention to lodge what he claimed was a record of the exchanges between Sinn Féin and his government in the British parliament. But, before he could do so, on Monday morning 29 November 1993 the Sinn Féin negotiating team publicly produced our account of the meetings and of the documents that were exchanged. Embarrassingly for the British, when the media compared the British and Sinn Féin versions, the British version was quickly exposed as inaccurate. Subsequently, on 1 December Mayhew admitted that a number of errors had emerged in the British account. He claimed twenty-two in all. This further reinforced the already widespread view that the Sinn Féin account was true.

My first meeting with Mayhew took place in Washington in May 1995. President Clinton had organised an economic conference to boost the peace process. It proved impossible for the British, who had been trying to prevent Mayhew meeting with the Sinn Féin leadership, not to agree to a meeting at the conference. It was a very surreal meeting. There was no coffee, tea or anything stronger. Just a quick handshake – in private, no cameras – and a fifteen-minute meeting. Mayhew, using a written speaking note, told us why the British government would not allow Sinn Féin into all-party negotiations. He was visibly shaking and nervous as he spoke, and he stuck rigidly to the text of his note, which the British issued afterwards, almost word for word, as a public statement. I met Mayhew several times after that. He loosened up a wee bit, but under his and John Major's intransigent stewardship, the IRA cessation of military operations collapsed and the opportunity for progress stalled.

Mayhew was followed by Mo Mowlam, who was secretary of state from May 1997 until October 1999. She was an entirely different character. She is generally fondly remembered by all of us who knew her. She was smart and funny and willing to listen. Her battle against ill health is well known. Her famous wig – which she would throw on the table at the start of a conversation – was a great device for disarming even the most outraged politician. But like all of her predecessors and successors, Mo was in the North to defend British interests. Though these changed slightly under the then Prime Minister, Tony Blair, she did her job.

On one occasion, we discovered that the car Martin McGuinness and I were using to attend secret meetings was bugged. It was a stupid move by the British – a breach of good faith – and was authorised by Mo Mowlam. But she had a good heart. She also authorised funding for Bunscoil Phobal Feirste – an Irish-language primary school in west Belfast – despite huge resistance from within the Department of Education. She gave former British military bases back to local communities and supported the development of the Black and Divis mountains as a public amenity, alongside numerous other very important little things.

I spent my Sunday mornings or Saturday afternoons walking the garden at Hillsborough Castle with her – and her predecessors and successors – trying to get as much progress as possible, while also impressing upon them the need for an end to the union and partition.

Those that came after Mowlam brought their own personalities, competencies and biases with them. Whether Peter Mandelson, Peter Hain or Theresa Villiers, all were first and foremost Britain's pro-consuls – defending British interests on the island of Ireland. Before they arrived most were also relatively unknown – certainly in Ireland. Few here had ever heard of Francis Pym or Roy Mason or Peter Brooke. Many were never heard of again.

And now we have James Brokenshire. Who, I hear you ask? And truth be told, I don't know. Once again a British politician – who has no stake in this island – is given influence over our lives by a British government whose priority interests are not ours.

And so it goes on. And so it should end.

The Brexit referendum vote is just one more example of this. The Conservative government in London is committed to leaving the EU. The people of the North rejected it. All of this is an argument for an end to the union with Britain and for new relationships on the island of Ireland in which our priorities or interests are what will dictate policy.

It's Time to Stop

9 April 2011

Ronan Kerr was murdered on Saturday 2 April 2011 outside his home in Omagh, in Co. Tyrone. He was the second member of the Police Service of Northern Ireland (PSNI) to be killed by so-called dissident republican groups. I have met many people since then. Most have been former republican prisoners and their families and other activists of long standing. These are the stalwarts who over decades of conflict lost loved ones to the British Army, RUC and collusion, were tortured, imprisoned and had their homes raided and often wrecked. They were and are the people who have been the backbone of the republican struggle over many years and they have suffered grievously for their stand against British injustice and partition. And they are seething with anger at the violent actions of a small core of anti-peace groups who have killed citizens, forced the elderly from their homes, injured children, threatened community workers, orchestrated sectarian conflict at interfaces and some of whom are involved in extortion and drug-related crime.

I want once more to address these groups directly. Sinn Féin has offered – through people like me and Martin McGuinness – to meet you and to outline our strategy for advancing republican and democratic objectives and our belief in the futility of armed actions. So far you have refused to speak to us, dismissed us and placed a death threat on some of us. Despite this I make the same offer again. I have no problem with anyone disagreeing with Sinn Féin. That is your right, but you have no right to attack anyone and there is no support for this. That is clear from the overwhelming public rejection of the attack that killed Ronan Kerr. The people of this island demand that you stop. I am prepared to meet you anywhere, at any time, to listen to what you have to say and to tell you that there is now a democratic, peaceful way to unite our people and our country on the basis of equality. Your achievement has only been to unite us all in opposition to your actions. It is time to end these futile attacks on the peace process; they will not succeed.

I would also like to address the small number of people who might have some tolerance for armed actions. To those who might shelter or provide resources and facilities to the perpetrators of these actions you need to ask yourselves what purpose is being served? Don't be fooled into thinking that you are helping the IRA. The war is over. The IRA is gone. The IRA embraced, facilitated and supported the peace process. When a democratic and peaceful alternative to armed struggle was created, the IRA left the stage. Those who murdered Ronan Kerr are not the IRA. Those who murdered Ronan Kerr have no coherent strategy. Your actions do not advance republican objectives. In fact, they advance no political agenda whatsoever.

Moreover, as has happened in many other conflict resolution processes, some of those who were formerly engaged in conflict turn their hand to criminality, or those who are purely criminal exploit the situation for their own ends. This is not a new phenomenon, nor is it uniquely Irish. However, some of these people who are masquerading as activists and others who support violent anti-peace actions are heavily involved in extortion, robberies and tiger kidnappings in republican heartlands. Sinn Féin is totally committed to exposing these activities and to taking a stand against them.

What is remarkable at this time is that no one is articulating any defence or explanation or rationale for these actions. Where are the political groups who criticise Sinn Féin and vent their anger at our strategy? Some of these groups, or individuals associated with them – a small number – are standing in local government elections in the North. They should be challenged on these issues.

Irish republicanism was always about more than militarism. You claim to be republican but your actions are anti-republican and against peace. You are unrepresentative of the community and do not define republicanism. You are not dissidents; dissent is a good and necessary part of any democratic or social movement. Through a long and hard process of negotiation, effort and hard work, Sinn Féin developed a peace strategy and, with others, created a peace process that has brought about fundamental and positive change. Significant progress has been made, although this is a continuing struggle.

One example of this is the fact that in May 2011 there will be an election to the power-sharing Assembly and Executive at the end of a successful four-year term. Who could have imagined twenty years ago that Martin McGuinness would be in government with Ian Paisley or Peter Robinson, and that there would be a power-sharing system involving Sinn Féin, the DUP and other parties? Who could have imagined the all-Ireland institutions that are working and delivering for citizens and each day making the border more and more irrelevant? Who could have imagined that Irish republicanism would be in the vanguard of change? The largest nationalist party in the North, with ministers in an Executive and fourteen newly elected TDs in the Dáil? Almost 400,000 citizens have voted for Sinn Féin in the last twelve months; more than voted for Fianna Fáil. This is evidence of the growth and strength of real republican politics. This is progress and it should be developed.

The Good Friday Agreement provides a peaceful and demo-cratic means to achieve republican objectives for those who have such goals. In the referendum held after the Good Friday Agreement, when the vast majority of citizens North and South voted for the agreement, and in every subsequent election when they have voted for pro-agreement parties, the people of this island have voted for the Good Friday Agreement and the subsequent agreements.

There is a huge onus on mainstream political parties and civic and church leaders to go beyond the politics of condemnation. The Irish government in particular, along with the Executive, have a solemn responsibility to fully implement all aspects of the Good Friday and subsequent agreements. The Irish government in particular has a responsibility as a co-equal partner with the British government, to ensure that London fulfils all of its responsibilities. This will require a step change in Dublin's approach to these matters. It is also of huge importance that the response to the actions of these anti-peace process groups is entirely within the law and human rights compliant.

There is no excuse, justification or explanation that can validate the murder of Ronan Kerr or any of the other actions of those involved in his killing. Our goal in the time ahead must be to defend the peace process and the Good Friday Agreement. Sinn Féin believes that the conditions which in the past led to republican armed actions have fundamentally changed. Political conditions have changed. New opportunities now exist to advance republican goals. I, along with others in the Sinn Féin leadership, am willing to discuss all of this with any prepared to speak to us.

IRISH AMERICA

Happy St Patrick's Day

I am on the train from New York to Washington DC. The train is a very good way to travel, particularly in the USA as they have a quiet car. Use of mobile phones is banned. So is talking. 'Absolutely no conversation,' declares the conductor in a tone which has a sense of authority that will not brook any deviation from her orders. I am used to women bossing me about so, as a stranger in a strange land, I am quietly reassured by her presence.

Before my train journey I made my way into the Franciscan Church off Seventh Avenue. It was filled with people and the mass was in Korean. Not surprisingly, the congregation were mostly Koreans and they sang like angels. They also bowed to each other at appropriate times during the ceremony. I wasn't long catching on. Between the bowing and the singing and the loud applause at the end, the Korean mass was a nice experience.

Anyway, back on the train. The woman conductor with the bossy voice is called Eileen. Her people come from Co. Cavan. The USA is like that. Paddies everywhere and not just on St Patrick's Day. One of the privileges of my work is to get to meet with some of these people who give of their time and money, even in recessionary times, to assist the Irish cause. I met some of them this morning and will meet more this evening and tomorrow – St Patrick's Day will be spent in Washington – and on Wednesday and Thursday I will be up in Boston before the long journey home. These trips are always exhausting, but they are uplifting as well. To engage with people and organisations who care deeply about Ireland and the Irish people is inspiring and very worthwhile.

Irish America still has considerable clout here. The Speakers Lunch and the reception in the White House is evidence of that. President Obama has his hands full with domestic issues, the recession and two wars but it is expected that he will take time to commit support to the Irish peace process and almost certain that he will announce the name of the new Special Envoy. All that is good.

I also expect a positive announcement from Tom DiNapoli, the New York State Comptroller, on the investment front. That is good also. Martin McGuinness and Peter Robinson did some productive work here on the west coast so that should lead to positive news as well. Not bad for the recessionary times that are in it.

Let us be vigilant. But let us continue to set an entirely positive and worthy agenda all day, every day in the mighty work of uniting the people of our small island and ending British rule in our country.

That's the journey we are on and as surely as this train is eating up the miles between New York and Washington we also will reach that destination. In the meantime, I am going for a little shut-eye. My jetlag has jetlag. Have a good St Patrick's Day. *Zzzzzzzzzz.*

A Good Day's Work

15 June 2009

'This is an assembly of the Irish–American community' one delegate declared to the large gathering in the Hilton Hotel in New York on Saturday 13 June 2009. 'And what a community we are.'

I agree. The community that filled the Hilton in its myriad social and campaigning groups – 800 activists in all from the east coast of the USA – were all crowded into the large downtown hotel to plot a course forward in support of Irish unity. Renowned writer Pete Hamill chaired proceedings and Professor Brendan O'Leary, American Labour leader Terry O'Sullivan and former Beirut hostage Brian Keenan made contributions that were both informative and instructive before the 'assembly' went into plenary session.

It was a great event. For those who don't follow these matters, the New York conference has it origins in a task force on Irish unity that I established in 2008. It also recognised the status of Irish unity as an international issue and put forward a number of suggestions to mobilise international opinion behind this proposition. Engagement with the Irish diaspora is a first step in such a process. That's what the gathering was about. The participants seemed uplifted and energised by the proceedings.

They heard Professor O'Leary of the University of Pennsylvania outline some of the ways to unite Ireland. Interestingly he also pointed out that the Scottish Nationalist Party's recent victory over the British Labour Party could bring an end to the union of England and Scotland in the quite near future. The SNP took 29 per cent of the Scottish vote in the European elections in June 2009, pushing the Labour Party into a humiliating second place on 20.8 per cent with the Tories on 16.8 per cent. If this trend continued it would have obvious ramifications for the so-called United Kingdom and the Good Friday Agreement part in which we live.[1]

Brian Keenan's contribution to the assembly was worth the trip in itself. He held the audience spellbound with his account of growing up in unionist east Belfast. In his evocative use of language Brian painted very vivid pictures, poetic and haunting in turn, of the mindsets of that section of our people who are cultural unionists, particularly the working-class section. I found his contribution very revealing and moving.

Terry O'Sullivan, general president of the Labourers International Union of North America, is a very successful, innovative and progressive organiser, who outlined to the conference how activists could organise. He also promised his support and the backing of other prominent leaders of organisations for the campaign.

Lots of ideas came out of the plenary session. The broadest consensus for activism was around the notion of a MacBride Principles-type campaign. This would involve gathering resolutions of support at local, city, state and federal level as a means of winning political support for the issue and putting it on the Congressional and Administration's agenda.

---

1   A Scottish referendum on independence did of course occur on 18 September 2014, with the Scottish people voting by 55.3 per cent to 44.7 per cent to remain in the UK. Subsequently, in the Westminster general election of 2017, the issue of a possible second referendum – which the SNP strongly campaigned for – appears to have led to a drop in the SNP share of the vote from 50 per cent to 36.9 per cent. The pro-union parties saw their vote increase. The Conservative Party increased their share to 28.6 per cent and Labour took 27.1 per cent of the vote. How this will impact on the battle for a second referendum is not yet clear.

Interestingly, US Senator Chuck Schumer and Congress member Eliot Engel dropped by and there were messages of support from many other public officials and representatives. Of course, the conference is only a part of the process, the real work begins – or continues – in the time ahead. I am confident that it will be successful. When Irish America gets its teeth into an issue, it delivers. It did with the MacBride Principles Campaign, which saw many states across the USA support the MacBride Principles for fair employment in the North. These were a set of principles used to govern US investment in companies employing citizens in the North, the purpose of which was to guard against discrimination. It did so in the infancy of the peace process and in the developing situation since then.

Some of the people in the assembly in the Hilton are experienced activists from that era. Some are new recruits. All have one thing in common: a belief in their ability to make a difference and establish a connection to Ireland that is uplifting and refreshing. I learned a lot from Saturday's assembly. I also learned a lot from a session with Brian Keenan and Terry Anderson as they broke bread with us afterwards and talked over their time in captivity in Beirut. It was almost like being at a Cage Eleven reunion.

The Continuum

Saturday 19 March 2011 was a cold, sharp day in New York. I travelled to Calvary Cemetery in Woodside in the borough of Queens to attend a commemoration in memory of the 1981 hunger strikers. Over the years I have been in many such places. But Calvary is on a different scale to anything I have ever experienced before. It is huge. It is so big that it is divided into four parts and together they hold over three million souls.

Calvary Cemetery was established in 1847 and opened the following year. It is said that there were fifty burials a day and that half were Irish, mostly victims of *An Gorta Mór* – The Great Hunger. They were some of the hundreds of thousands of Irish men and women and children who had fled starvation and poverty in Ireland for the New World, only to catch cholera or some other illness. They died in fever camps and ports the length of Canada and the USA.

The commemoration for the hunger strikers was fittingly at the Patriots' Plot. A large Celtic cross marks the spot where the Irish Republican Brotherhood (IRB) decided to open a republican plot in 1907. It is dedicated to the memory of those who rose in rebellion against the British during the Fenian campaign in 1867. Although that rising failed, the IRB stayed true. For decades it planned and organised. Nine years after the Patriots' Plot was opened, the IRB was at the heart of the Easter Rising of 1916, the Proclamation of the Republic and the formation of the IRA.

Larry Downes, who is the President of Friends of Sinn Féin in the USA, gave me an old report from *The New York Times* of the burial of John Neary. He was the first to be buried in the Patriots' Plot. But Neary's connections with republican struggle predate even the Fenian Rising. He was involved also in the abortive rising of the Young Irelanders in 1848 and, after that, like many hundreds of thousands of others of his generation after the Great Hunger, he was forced to leave Ireland.

Many went to the USA, while others were scattered around the globe and many moved to England. John Neary was one of those who travelled to England, where he remained a committed and active Fenian. In 1867 he was involved in planning the escape of Thomas Kelly and Timothy Deasy, two leading Fenian activists, as they were being taken to prison in Manchester. Kelly and Deasy escaped but three of those involved in helping them – William Philip Allen, Michael Larkin and Michael O'Brien: the Manchester Martyrs – were executed as a result of the killing of a policeman during the escape.

Many of those involved in that escape later made their way to the USA and were present in Calvary Cemetery when John Neary was finally laid to rest forty years later. The Patriots' Plot, and those who lie there, are a reminder of the long continuum of the struggle for freedom in Ireland. They also symbolise the hugely significant role that the Irish in America have played down through the centuries in assisting that struggle.

The 1916 Proclamation makes this connection explicit:

> ... having resolutely waited for the right moment to reveal itself, she now seizes that moment, and, supported by her exiled children in America ...

Men like Joe McGarrity and Clan na Gael played a crucial role in funding the Rising and then providing arms and political support during the Tan War. After partition and the disastrous Civil War, once again many republicans were forced to leave Ireland and they went to the USA. But they never forgot their homeland.

In 1969, when the most recent phase of conflict erupted, Irish America stepped forward and again provided invaluable support for the oppressed people in the North and for the struggle. The Clan and NORAID and a host of other organisations came forward to help prisoners and their families, brought children to the USA for holidays away from the conflict and lobbied US leaders to oppose British policy in Ireland. A very effective information campaign, often spontaneous, ensured that British propaganda was challenged. And there were some also who, as in previous generations, gave direct support and assistance to those engaged in armed actions – the IRA.

One consequence of the conflict in the 1970s was the attempt by the British to criminalise the prisoners and, through them, the struggle for freedom. In 1980 the men in the H-Blocks and women in Armagh embarked on the first hunger strike. On 1 March 1981 the second hunger strike commenced, of which Bobby Sands was the first hunger striker.

I reminded a large crowd of Irish-Americans that on that day thirty years previously Bobby was on the nineteenth day of his hunger strike. Two days earlier, on St Patrick's Day 1981, Bobby concluded the secret prison diary that he had been keeping. His last words in that diary on 17 March are a reminder of the spirit and resolve of the Irish people over many centuries to achieve freedom:

> If they aren't able to destroy the desire for freedom, they won't break you. They won't break me because the desire for freedom, and the freedom of the Irish people, is in my heart. The day will dawn when all the people of Ireland will have the desire for freedom to show. It is then we'll see the rising of the moon.

Bobby died on hunger strike along with his nine comrades: Francie Hughes, Raymond McCreesh, Patsy O'Hara, Joe McDonnell, Martin Hurson, Kevin Lynch, Kieran Doherty, Tom McElwee and Mickey Devine. Their courage and self-sacrifice caught the imagination of Irish-American activists, who rallied in their tens of thousands in support of the prisoners. The extraordinary courage of the prisoners gave strength to the struggle and the hunger strike was a watershed moment in Irish history. Irish America played a key role in that and subsequently in the efforts to build the peace process.

So, those buried in the Patriots' Plot in Calvary Cemetery, 3,000 miles from home, played their part. It is right that as republicans in Ireland remember the hunger strikers, and all those who gave their lives in pursuit of freedom, we also remember those who went before them and who died in the far-flung corners of the world.

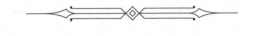

INTERNATIONAL

A Great Moment

26 January 2009

Billions of words have probably been written and spoken about the inauguration of Barack Obama. The television coverage drew multitudes around the globe. Since I've come back to Ireland from the inauguration everyone asks me: 'What was it like?'

What was it like? It was great. Not just the speeches or the hoopla or the sense of occasion. For me the biggest and most significant aspect of that big and significant event was the people. Some of them were on the train from New York to Washington: elderly African-American ladies with packed lunches and woolly hats to ward off the cold; old white guys with Obama badges on their backpacks; young kids of all ethnic backgrounds.

In Ireland there would have been a sing-song. Here there was a quiet undercurrent of excitement. When the train disembarked at Union Station – along with trains from all over the USA – the stream of passengers became part of an ocean of humanity making its way to the exits. By now the sense of excitement and good humour and expectation was palpable. Like an All-Ireland Sunday.

By fluke Richard McAuley, Joseph Smith and I found ourselves next to George Mitchell. I dunted – or, as they say within the Pale, shouldered – him gently. He turned in surprise.

'Of all the gin joints in all the world, Gerry,' he exclaimed.

I meant to ask him about the media speculation that he was to get the Middle East job. But he was there with his clann and in the good-natured jostling and pushing I forgot.

It was 'chaos' outside the station. Organised, cheerful chaos.

There were cops everywhere – and firemen. The roads around the station were chock full of people. Our hotel was the same. And early next morning at the American Legion Club adjacent to Capitol Hill where we were to meet our host congressman, Richard Neal, it was the same. As we chatted with Richie's other guests, the plasma television screen showed images of Barack and Michelle Obama going into church. He waved at the cameras. The small group of grizzled African-American veterans seated before the TV screen burst into applause. Watching them I felt the tears well in my eyes.

And then it was out onto the sidewalk led by the intrepid Billy Tranghese, who works as chief of staff for Richie Neal. Two hours later, accompanied by Dave and Chris Kearney and Mike and Barbara Ashe from Springfield, Massachusetts, in Congressman Neal's district and formerly of the Blasket Islands, I was in our designated area. Richard and Joseph had long ago left me. They, irony of ironies, were in the Orange Area. I didn't care. I was to be in the seated area in Section 11. But when we arrived the seated area was packed and the passageway soon filled up.

'Sit down, sit down,' the people in the seats chorused cheerfully.

'Give us back our seats,' the standing crowd chorused cheerfully back at them.

All the while huge screens beamed out images of former presidents, first ladies and other notables. Some were booed. But every time the Obama clann appeared the crowd cheered. I made my way through the throng with my Co. Kerry compatriots. A very good-natured usher entreated us all to sit down. As our seats were taken I had to hitch up my long johns, cast my Aran hat before me on the frosty ground and kneel on it. As I did so the sun came out, the breeze disappeared and the San Francisco Boys and Girls Chorus began to sing.

The next singer was Aretha Franklin. She sang 'My Country,

'Tis of Thee'. Marian Anderson had sung that song seventy years ago at the Lincoln Memorial, having been banned from performing in *The Daughters of American Revolution's Constitution Hall* because of her skin colour. Ms Franklin was in fine voice from where I genuflected, a beat away from her. But the air of 'My Country, 'Tis of Thee' was vaguely familiar. I knew I had heard it before. It was the same as 'God Save The Queen'. That put me off momentarily. I was glad I wasn't standing. Unlike Richard and Joseph. In the Orange Area.

Joe Biden's swearing in passed without incident and to loud applause. John Williams' composition that followed on strings and clarinet contained elements of what seemed to me to be *Lord of the Dance*. It also passed without incident. Apparently it was mimed.

Barack Obama's swearing in wasn't mimed, however, and I was reassured when the Lord Chief Justice stumbled over the words. Been there, done that. It keeps you grounded. When they concluded the swearing in, the crowd – including myself – exploded with tumultuous cheers, amens and wild applause.

And then the new president made his speech and ushered in a new era in American and hopefully world politics. We were all on our feet as Elizabeth Alexander's poem cast magic word pictures into the bright, sunshiny day.

The Rev. Dr Joseph E. Lowery, considered the dean of the civil rights movement in the USA, and compatriot of Martin Luther King, gave the benediction. He knew his day had come. He drew loud amens and louder chuckles with his:

> May the white embrace right.
> May the brown be around.
> May the yellow be mellow.
> May the redman be the headman.

One US national anthem later and that was it. It was a great moment in our shared history.

What did it all mean?

The cynics will say 'very little'.

But cynics don't believe. To believe you have to set aside disbelief. Cynics can't do that. Cynics are giver uppers.

The fact is the majority of the electorate in the USA voted for positive change. They elected an African-American. That is significant in itself. But they also elected an African-American – a US president – who promises positive change.

The world needs change. We know that. Real change. In Ireland. In the USA. Everywhere. It's been a long time coming.

But we can hope. And I do. And we can wish the new US president well. And I do that also.

Twenty Years a Growing

10 November 2009

On 9 November 1989 the Berlin Wall came down. I remember watching the scenes of jubilation on television. This evening's television news revisited those scenes of euphoria and jubilation twenty years on. The great and the good are gathered at the Brandenburg Gate for the formal celebrations.

It is interesting to see Mikhail Gorbachev, former secretary-general of the Communist Party of the Soviet Union, alongside other world leaders of that period. Until his reign, the Kremlin had intervened militarily to stifle dissent, most famously in Hungary in 1956 and, in my memory, in Prague in 1968, when Soviet tanks moved in to bring an end to the efforts to establish a democratic government.

At that time I was working in the Duke of York public house in downtown Belfast. The Duke was the watering hole and eating house for Belfast union leaders, Labour Party types, the Communist Party leadership and a scattering of Republican leaders. Our own civil rights struggle was starting to assert itself but I have clear recollections of how discussions among Belfast's 'Left', or at least 'the Left' as represented in the Duke, was galvanised by the events on the streets of Prague. But for all the soul-searching and heated-but-intelligent debate, no one predicted that a brief few decades later the Soviet Union would be no more.

Gorbachev certainly was about reforming and modernising the Soviet Union, and not about ending it. In the 1980s when the Polish trade union Solidarity organised across Poland there was no repeat of the Prague crackdown. By the summer of 1988 hefty hikes in food prices led to strikes across Poland. Before long negotiations dealt with political as well as social and economic matters. Hungary followed. My guess is that the bulk of the protestors, at the start at least, wanted only to improve their systems, not to overthrow them, although, and this is another guess, I'm sure many became more ambitious and more radical as they became more politicised. And more successful.

I am also sure the masses of people assembled in Berlin for the celebrations include many of the people who participated in the momentous events that led to the walls coming down. Of course young Germans – twenty-somethings – will have no memory of the 'Wall'. Maybe their parents or grandparents were activists. Maybe they were reared on stories of what things were like in a divided Germany and a separated Berlin. It must be an extremely emotional event for an activist to be at the Brandenburg Gate tonight with children or grandchildren and to be part of all that.

I wonder how history would have flowed if the border guards had opened fire on those brave people who first pushed their way through the border crossing that fateful day twenty years ago. Or if Thatcher's warnings against German unity had been heeded? But of course, she was wrong. Again. And not only on Ireland, though that is little consolation.

Then on 3 October 1990 Germany was reunited – irony of ironies – under an Irish presidency of the EU, with Charlie Haughey as EU president.

There have been acres of books written about why all this happened. It's simple, stoopid. It's called the human spirit. It has a way of overcoming all the odds. It can even destroy empires. And knock down walls. And reunite people and countries. And despite all the doomsday warnings and threats and concerns it seems that Germans are glad to be united. And why wouldn't they be?

From the limited dip I took into international news agencies' coverage of the celebrations, most young Germans are happy with their country. They take unity for granted. That is clear from a series of polls to coincide with the twentieth anniversary.

A bit like how Ireland's own young people will be at the twentieth anniversary of our own reunification.

Afghanistan and Ireland – Same Old Story!

31 July 2010

When I stood in the Guildhall Square in Derry on 15 June 2010 I watched as the relatives of the fourteen victims of the British Parachute Regiment expressed their delight at the Saville Report's conclusion, which stated that the fourteen people who died on 30 January 1972 while taking part in a civil rights march in Derry – a day referred to as 'Bloody Sunday' – were innocent victims. At the time the dead were labelled terrorists by the British government. The British system and, to its shame, much of the British media, accused those who had been shot of being 'gunmen' and 'bombers'. Lies were told, a cover-up concocted and the British establishment closed ranks to defend the actions of its army. That lie persisted for decades.

On the same day the report was published, British Prime Minister David Cameron, speaking in the British parliament, apologised for what happened. I am sure the words of regret and remorse he made that day were heartfelt and the people of Derry welcomed them. However, Mr Cameron then sought to expunge the violent record of the British Army in the North by claiming that: 'Bloody Sunday is not the defining story of the service the British Army gave in Northern Ireland from 1969–2007.'

He was wrong. Bloody Sunday did define the British Army's role in the North. As did the massacre in Ballymurphy six months earlier in August 1971, when the same regiment responsible for Bloody Sunday – the Paras – shot dead eleven innocent victims;

as did the Springhill murders five months later, in July 1972, when they shot dead five more. The victims were again accused of being 'gunmen' or in one case a 'gunwoman'.

On Friday 30 July 2010, in a welcome development, Catholic Bishop of Down and Connor Noel Treanor gave the families of the Ballymurphy Massacre victims archive documents, including eyewitness statements from church records of the time. They validate the families' position that those killed in Ballymurphy and Springhill were unarmed civilians.

The Ballymurphy and Springhill killings were par for the course for the British Army. In countless actions over decades of war the British Army and RUC strategy employed shoot-to-kill operations and other nefarious activities (plastic bullets; mass raids on homes; torture; curfews; intimidation; collusion between state forces and unionist death squads) to assassinate many hundreds of citizens and intimidate a whole community.

The full resources of the British state, including its legal, judicial and propaganda institutions, were brought to bear. It was claimed that victims were gunmen or women, whose weapons were spirited away by hostile crowds; or they were protestors who made actions which gave the soldiers cause to believe they were armed or a threat; or they ran away from patrols, justifying their being shot, while others were accused of attacking patrols or trying to run British soldiers down in cars. The truth is still denied by the British government to relatives in many of these cases.

It was also often said that the North was Britain's training ground for its military and intelligence system. Interrogation techniques, the use of computers, logging the movement of people, gathering intelligence and developing tactics for controlling a population were all part of the British Army's activities in the North. This also included media handling following the killing of civilians or accusations of torture.

The same techniques were then applied in Iraq and Afghanistan. Evidence of this emerged in some 90,000 US military files that were posted on the WikiLeaks website on 25 July 2010 and carried in detail in a number of newspapers, including the *Guardian*, *The New York Times* and *Der Spiegel*. The files are from a variety of NATO military sources operating in Afghanistan between 2004 and 2009, and they reveal a depth of failure of the NATO military strategy that has not heretofore been evident in the media's coverage of the war.

The Afghanistan experience, and the techniques and strategies and propaganda employed in that war, fit a pattern that will be familiar to people in Ireland and especially the North. The WikiLeaks documents provide evidence of previously unreported actions in which Afghan civilians were killed or wounded. In 144 incidents detailed almost 200 civilians were killed and hundreds more injured. This is almost certainly a serious underestimation of the true scale of civilian casualties.

The WikiLeaks files provide a list of actions involving the British Army. These are some:

5 November 2006: In Helmand [a province in southern Afghanistan] the British Army's Marine Commandos fired 'warning shots' at a vehicle, killed two civilians and wounded two others, including a child.

October/November 2007: A cluster of shootings by British soldiers in Kabul [capital city of Afghanistan] led to the death of the son of an Afghan general. The British soldiers are unidentified and the US report reveals that: 'Investigation controlled by the British. We are unable to get complete story.'

12 March 2008: Helmand. British troops call in gunships and claim three enemy dead. The bodies of two women and two children are later found.

19 November 2008: Marine Commandos fire 'warning shots' at a vehicle. They kill a child.

19 January 2009: Marine Commandos use a drone to attack the Taliban. Two children are wounded.

27 January 2009: Marine Commandos shoot at two people 'watching the patrol'. A man and a child are wounded.

19 May 2009: Ghurkhas [a unit composed of Nepalese Gurkha soldiers in the British Army] call in air strike and kill eight civilians and destroy a family compound.

30 September 2009: Helmand. The Rifles Regiment call in an air strike on a compound housing two families. Seven killed.

10 November 2009: Helmand. Coldstream Guards kill a driver of a vehicle.

When asked to respond to these accusations the British Ministry of Defence said: 'We are currently examining our records to establish the facts in the alleged casualty incidents raised.'

The British Army is not alone in carrying out these kinds of actions. French troops shot at a bus full of children, killing eight. A US patrol did the same and killed fifteen. In another incident, US Special Forces dropped six 2,000lb bombs on a compound, killing up to 300 people.

Human Rights Watch, which reported on the war in the North of Ireland and is now doing similar work in Afghanistan, said: 'These files bring to light what's been a consistent trend by US and NATO forces: the concealment of civilian deaths.' Also revealed is the existence of Taskforce 373 – a covert operations unit whose task is to 'remove' the enemy.

All of this just scratches the surface of another dirty war that is being fought using modern versions of old strategies and techniques, and is once again failing. Will the publication of the battlefield and intelligence documents by WikiLeaks make a difference? 'None,' according to the British Foreign Secretary William Hague. His retort could just as easily have come from the mouth of Reginald Maudling or William Whitelaw or Roy Mason or Tom King or any of the previous British ministers who had responsibility for the British war in Ireland and whose policies sustained a conflict that could have ended much earlier.

But then should we be surprised? Should those of us who survived be taken aback by the stupidity of the British military and political mind? A former commander of the British Army in Afghanistan, Colonel Richard Kemp, recently claimed that the British Army won the war in Ireland. If Colonel Kemp, who presumably was the British Army's key strategist in Afghanistan, could get it so wrong in our country, why should anyone expect him to get it right in Afghanistan? And if he and William Hague are reflective of British thinking today, then the British are destined to make the same mistakes in that part of the world as they made here.

Somalia – A Failure of Politics

25 July 2011

Imagine walking from Belfast to Dublin or from Derry to Cork!

Imagine doing it in your bare feet.

Imagine walking in the scorching heat and with no water and food.

Imagine carrying your children and being forced to leave some of them lying dead at the side of the road because you haven't the strength to dig a hole to bury them.

Imagine a landscape blasted by heat, with sparse vegetation and the rotting remains of cattle and other animals dead of thirst – a harsh and unforgiving countryside.

Imagine that those around you are empty-eyed and gaunt with swollen and extended stomachs.

This is the reality of life and death for hundreds of thousands of men, woman and children. It is the immediate future for millions more. It is Somalia.

Famine is a terrible word. It conjures up frightening images, particularly for many in Ireland given the folk memory of the Great Hunger of the 1840s.

The Horn of Africa today, like much of Africa, is still conflicted by the brutal legacy of colonisation. It is also caught up in the post 9/11 international conflict with Islamist groups linked to al-Qaeda. Climate change may be playing its part but it is the decisions of past colonial governments, as well as the policies being pursued by the international community and local indigenous governments, including a Somali government whose remit extends only a few kilometres beyond the Somali capital,

Mogadishu, which have created this crisis. Ultimately it is a failure of politics.

No one will be surprised that the areas worst affected correlate to those which suffer the most entrenched deprivation and poverty, where there has been an absence of investment in infrastructure, health programmes, agricultural training, education for children and jobs. Somalia, northern Kenya and southern Ethiopia are experiencing their worst drought in sixty years. This has had a disastrous impact on the largely pastoral and farming communities living in the affected area.

Ten million people are affected by the famine. That is almost twice the population of Ireland. It's the first time in almost twenty years that the word famine has been used to describe the conditions in Somalia. Every day hungry, thirsty, tired and emaciated figures make their way in slow processions through a blistered, dying landscape towards hastily erected refugee camps. Dadaab in north-east Kenya has almost 400,000 people crammed within its increasing boundaries. That's more people than live in the city of Belfast totally dependent on international aid. The 4,000 people living in a refugee camp called 'Safety' on the outskirts of Mogadishu have built their homes out of plastic sheets, wood and branches. People sleep on the ground.

The horror stories now being reported by the media tell the desperate story of people on the edge of disaster. One account recorded the experience of Amina, who had walked fifty kilometres with her one-and-a-half-year-old son on her back only to discover when she arrived at 'Safety' that he was dead.

The UN defines famine as:

- More than 30 per cent of children suffering from acute malnutrition.

- Two adults or four children dying of hunger each day for every group of 10,000 people.

- The population must have less than 2,100 calories of food each day.

In the famine-affected areas of Bakool in south-west Somalia and Lower Shabelle in the south, the reality is already far worse than this. Aid is needed immediately. But the bomb and gun attacks on 22 July 2011 at a summer camp on the island of Utøya in Norway by Anders Behring Breivik, a right-wing extremist, and the death of Amy Winehouse have pushed this issue off the media agenda. This reduces the political momentum for the urgent intervention essential to save lives.

The UN Food Agency is holding crisis talks on the issue in Rome and there have been pledges of money for famine aid, but thus far it is insufficient to meet the immediate needs of those millions at risk and it is inadequate in building the necessary infrastructure to minimise the threat of famine in the future.

More needs to be done and quickly.

Addendum

Six years later the people of Somalia face the same challenges they confronted in 2011. At least twenty million men, women and children are facing immediate starvation in the famine-affected areas. While drought is playing its part in the catastrophe, it is widely accepted that this is largely a man-made famine, exacerbated by civil war, government policy and the actions of groups like Al-Shabaab in Somalia, which are blocking aid workers from getting to communities in trouble.

The Basque Country

Monday 17 October 2011 was a busy day and hopefully a significant one for the people of the Basque country and Spain. It started with a plane flight to Bilbao from Dublin. A Sinn Féin delegation met up with former Taoiseach Bertie Ahern at Dublin Airport. Bertie and I were going to the Basque country as part of an international panel of political leaders. We joined Jonathan Powell, former chief of staff to Tony Blair, on board a small plane bound for a conference in San Sebastian in Euskadi (the Basque name for the area) entitled: 'International conference to promote the resolution of the conflict in the Basque Country'. The event had been organised by a range of groups, including the Basque Citizens' Network for Agreement and Consultation, Lokarri; the International Contact Group (ICG) led by South African lawyer Brian Currin; and four other international foundations.

We were due to join up with former UN Secretary General Kofi Annan, Pierre Joxe, the former French Defence and Interior Minister, and Gro Harlem Brundtland, a former Norwegian Prime Minister. The flight took about two hours and provided Bertie, Jonathan and us with an opportunity to talk about the conference.

The format was straightforward. Each of the six international participants would make a contribution on the issue of conflict resolution, its difficulties and hopes. A range of trade union, business, community and political representatives from the Basque country would then make short presentations. After that the international guests would retire to discuss and agree a

'Declaration', which would set out our view of how the process of peace in the Basque country could be advanced.

I have been in the Basque country many times in recent years. There is a long affinity between Irish people and the people of France and Spain and the Basque country. Sinn Féin's efforts to assist in building a peace process there go back to the Good Friday Agreement. In that time there have been moments of great hope but also of despair as the opportunity for peace suffered setbacks.

I was in the Basque country in June 2006 after the separatist group ETA called a cessation to their armed campaign. There was great excitement and anticipation. The collapse of the cessation at the end of that year was a disappointment to many. Since then Sinn Féin has continued to work closely with our Basque friends in Batasuna – the Basque nationalist political party, which is currently banned – and others, in an effort to inject new momentum into a peace process that is stalled.

In the last two years we have seen the formation of Abertzale Left, a coalition of left and nationalist-leaning parties that includes Batasuna, and the adoption in February 2010 of a new political strategy for progress. The example of the Irish peace process is clear in this strategy as it commits Abertzale Left to using exclusively political and democratic means to advance its political objectives. It seeks to advance political change in a complete absence of violence and without interference, conducted in accordance with the Mitchell Principles. And its political goal is to achieve a stable and lasting peace in the Basque country.

Subsequently, ETA called a new ceasefire in September 2010 and last month saw the establishment of the International Commission of Verification of Ceasefire in the Basque Country – Comisión Internacional de Verificación (CIV).

So Monday's initiative in San Sebastian is rooted in a lot of hard work and effort and some progress. There was and is an expectation that the conference could see a significant change in the situation. That was certainly the expectation among those taking part in the conference in the Ghandi room in the San Sebastian Peace House and among the ranks of journalists who were covering it.

In my contribution to the conference I recalled that for many the conflict in Ireland, rooted in centuries of war and division and violence, had seemed intractable. Every generation had known war – and between the cycles of violence there was the despair of oppression and discrimination, of instability and institutional violence. The cycle seemed destined to continue into a depressing future. But the Irish peace process demonstrated that with imagination, dialogue and a commitment to achieving peace it is possible to rewrite the script. I said: 'Violence usually occurs when people believe that there is no alternative. Transforming a situation from conflict to peace requires, therefore, that an alternative is created.'

Making peace is hugely challenging and enormously difficult. It demands that we seek to understand what motivates, what inspires, what drives opponents. Ultimately, as Madiba – Nelson Mandela – said, we have to make friends with our enemy. Each conflict is different, but in the course of our efforts Irish republicans have learned that there are general principles of peacemaking and methods of conflict resolution that can be applied elsewhere and which can help end conflict if applied properly. These elements include: dialogue; tackling the causes which lie at the heart of the conflict; a good faith engagement by all sides; an inclusive process – with all parties treated as equals and all mandates respected. All issues must be on the agenda. There can be no preconditions, no vetoes, no attempt to predetermine the outcome or preclude any outcome, and there should be time frames.

Most importantly, participants must stay focused and be

prepared to take risks and engage in initiatives and confidence-building measures. But if there is a starting point, it must be dialogue. I emphasised this again and again. This is the foundation upon which any progress will be built.

Confidence-building measures are also crucial. In Ireland this meant, among other things, improving conditions for prisoners, including moving those who were in England closer to their homes in Ireland. It meant demilitarising the environment and ending the use of emergency laws and repression, a new beginning to policing and the release of political prisoners. It also meant respecting and acknowledging the democratic rights of all political parties and treating them as equals. At a time when the Batasuna political party is banned and leaders like Arnaldo Otegi, who, in my view, is totally committed to peace, are imprisoned, the use of confidence-building measures by the Spanish state is very important.

At the end of our four hours of deliberation, the international delegation presented our 'Declaration'. We first read it to the conference and then went outside to the grounds of the Peace House where the media were camped. The 'Declaration' said that we believed it was possible to end the last armed confrontation in Europe. We set out a five-point proposal:

- We call upon ETA to make a public declaration of the definitive cessation of all armed action and to request talks with the governments of Spain and France to address exclusively the consequences of the conflict.

- If such a declaration is made we urge the governments of Spain and France to welcome it and agree to talks exclusively to deal with the consequences of the conflict.

- We urge that major steps be taken to promote reconciliation;

recognise, compensate and assist all victims; recognise the harm that has been done and seek to heal personal and social wounds.

- In our experience of resolving conflicts there are often other issues that, if addressed, can assist in the attainment of lasting peace. We suggest that non-violent actors and political representatives meet and discuss political and other related issues, in consultation with the citizenry, that could contribute to a new era without conflict. In our experience third-party observers or facilitators help such dialogue. Here, such dialogue could also be assisted by international facilitators, if that were desired by those involved.

- We are willing to form a committee to follow up these recommendations.

We urged the French and Spanish governments to respond positively and to agree to talks.

My colleagues and I said that we are willing to form a committee to follow up on our recommendations. There was applause from the media and with that, it was over. We said our goodbyes and got back into our cars for the return journey to Bilbao Airport. I think it was a good day's work.

As we made our way home, there was good news from another front. Tuesday 18 October saw the release of 477 Palestinian prisoners and of Israeli soldier Gilad Shalit, with another 550 Palestinian prisoners due to be released the following month. This is a welcome development. It came after talks involving the Netanyahu government and Hamas. It's wonderful what can happen when dialogue begins.

A Tale of Two Worlds

16 May 2012

This is a tale of two worlds – one rich and powerful, the other destitute and on the brink of the abyss.

The economic crisis in Europe and the impact of austerity policies in Greece, Spain, Portugal, Italy and in the Irish state are dominating the news agenda at this time. The talk is of billions of euro. Greece owes hundreds of billions. Spanish banks owe billions. The Irish government has given over €20 billion to bad banks to pay off private banking debt. French banks hold billions of euros of Greek debt – and are watching anxiously the unfolding crisis in that state. And then there is the European Financial Stability Facility with its €200 plus billion and the European Stability Mechanism which has €700 billion. Billions and billions and more billions. If it were not for the dire social consequences of the austerity policies, the reader could be forgiven for thinking this is all about Monopoly money.

A few hundred miles south of the EU there is another world – a wretched world of poverty and hunger where 220,000 children die each year from malnourishment and where one in five children will die before they reach the age of five. This place now faces its greatest threat. The Sahel region cuts a wide swathe across north Africa from the Atlantic Ocean in the west to the Red Sea in the east. The states that make up the area are already among the most impoverished countries in the world. Of the 187 states that make up the UN human development index Niger is ranked 186, Chad is 183, Burkina Faso 181 and Mali 175.

Today they face an unparalleled humanitarian disaster. The

Sahel has endured cyclical crises around food and water but usually this afflicts one or two states at any given time. This year at least eight states are affected and between fifteen and twenty-three million people are at grave risk, among them one million children and hundreds of thousands of pregnant women.

This crisis is not unexpected. In January the EU's Crisis Response Commissioner, Kristalina Georgieva, visited Niger and Chad and warned that 'we are running out of time'. Six months ago the UN World Food Programme was warning of a pending catastrophe. It identified the points of crisis, the states affected and the likely cost of dealing with this effectively. It estimated that it would need around $700 million. This is a large amount of money but it pales into insignificance when set against the billions being spoken of in Europe or the billions more in the budgets of the rich states that make up what is called the developed or first world. Thus far only about half the money needed by the UN has been received. The main aid agencies – World Vision, Action against Hunger, Save the Children and Oxfam – and others, like Concern, are urgently trying to raise money. But they currently have only achieved 20 per cent of their goal of $250 million.

The reports from the region are reminiscent of the accounts from Ireland at the time of the Great Hunger when the dead lay at the side of roads, their mouths green from eating grass. One World Food Programme worker described what he has recently witnessed in the Sahel:

> I've been to areas where some communities are reduced to eating wild plants, wild berries. Things that normally animals would eat. And they have no way of feeding themselves and their children. So you could say that technically in certain parts of the Sahel people are desperate and have nothing, literally nothing, left to eat but wild leaves.

An aid worker with World Vision described the situation in Mauritania, where many refugees from Mali have sought refuge. He said:

> People are arriving with nothing. They're living in camps which are just sheets on sticks with a few pots and pans. And there's a fierce wind blowing across the desert. The heat is unbearable. And so there we're able to see the extent of that suffering already playing out in those refugee camps.

The reasons for this crisis are many. Climate change and drought are important factors. So too are issues like poverty, population growth, poor government and political infrastructure and governance systems, a lack of money and the impact of several conflicts which have displaced hundreds of thousands of people. It is generally accepted that a significant cause for the latter was the conflict in Libya that saw many foreign workers from the Sahel forced to return home. This has led to a loss of income into already very poor areas and increased instability.

A conflict in Mali has seen an estimated 160,000 people forced to flee their homes into neighbouring states whose resources are at breaking point. Another 200,000 Malians have fled to other areas within the Mali state, adding to its crisis. All of this is contributing to an increasingly desperate situation.

In this tale of two worlds, there is an onus on the richer world – despite its economic difficulties – to reach down across the Mediterranean Sea and into the Sahel to provide the food and medicines and sustainable investment our neighbours need to live.

The EU, which is the biggest contributor of aid to the region, needs to do more, both in direct funding and in pushing individual EU states and other countries to contribute. But in the long term there is a more fundamental issue that must be addressed – how to build indigenous sustainable economic and agricultural systems that can meet the challenges of nature and man without whole populations being put at risk of starvation and disease.

Oireachtas Recognises the Palestinian State

11 December 2014

The Dáil concluded a two-day debate on a Sinn Féin motion calling for recognition of a Palestinian state and both houses of the Oireachtas now supports the right of the Palestinian people to self-determination, recognises a Palestinian state and endorses the Palestinian people's right to independence and sovereignty. This is a substantial and positive development that means Ireland is now a significant part of the consensus for peace and progress in the Middle East. It also means that Irish people are standing with progressive Israeli opinion, which wants a lasting peace arrangement and supports the recognition of a Palestinian state.

The passing of this motion, in conjunction with the passing of similar motions in parliaments across the EU, is an important act of solidarity with the Palestinian people. The dangers and the tensions in that tragic situation were underlined with the sad news yesterday (10 December 2014) of the death during a protest on the West Bank of Ziad Abu Ein, a cabinet minister in the Palestinian government. He died taking part in a non-violent demonstration to mark International Human Rights Day. He and others were planning to plant olive trees – symbols of peace – on land owned by a Palestinian but which, because of a nearby illegal Israeli settlement, is mostly off-limits to Palestinians. Palestinians claim that he died from a blockage in his coronary artery after being assaulted by Israeli soldiers during the protest. So now was exactly the right time for this motion.

I returned from the Middle East on Sunday 7 December 2014 having spent three days there. It was my fourth visit to the region in eight years. In 2009 I spent two days in Gaza. At that time the Israeli government wanted me to agree that I would not meet Hamas. If I refused they would deny me entry through the Erez crossing. I refused. I believe in dialogue. Israel relented and I spent forty-eight hours seeing for myself the devastating impact that the Israeli war of 2008–9 had on the people and infrastructure of Gaza. On this occasion, however, the Israeli government said no to my going into the Gaza Strip. It gave no explanation. An anonymous spokesperson later tried to claim it was because I wanted to 'hang out with Hamas' and because I wouldn't speak to the Israeli government. Neither claim is true.

I travelled into the West Bank. I spoke to President Abbas and others in the Palestinian Authority, to NGOs and representatives of Palestinian organisations, including Mustafa Barghouti of the Palestinian National Initiative. And in Jerusalem I met brave Israeli citizens deeply concerned for the future. Among them were Alon Liel and Ilan Baruch. Both are former professional diplomats in the Israeli government and both were ambassadors for Israel. They have been hugely critical of Israel's policy towards the Palestinian people and both support the campaign to secure official government recognition for a Palestine state by EU states and others. They share the belief of the Palestinian leadership that such a move will place the Palestinians and Israelis on an equal footing in any negotiations and create a new dynamic in the peace process. They also believe it is a right and principle that for too long has been conditional on the agreement of Israel.

Why should the right of the Palestinian people to sovereignty and statehood be dependent on Israel? Israel is a state. It has an embassy in Dublin and others scattered around the world. The Palestinians have a 'mission'. This is wrong. The people of Palestine have the right to freedom and independence and statehood. It should not be conditional on Israel or subject to any veto by it or any other state.

Alon Liel and his colleagues initiated a campaign in support of a Palestinian state. A letter, signed by over 900 prominent Israeli citizens, including Nobel laureates, writers, academics, business people and broadcasters, was sent to parliamentarians in Sweden, Britain, France, Spain, Belgium and in the Dáil, seeking support for a Palestinian state. All of these parliaments, now including the Oireachtas, passed positive motions of support.

The letter is evidence of a deep desire and hope by some Israelis to adopt an approach that they believe is in the interests of Palestinians but crucially is also in the interests of Israel. Those I met are proud patriotic Israelis. They believe the recognition of a Palestinian state is a key step on the road to ending the decades-long conflict. The letter reads:

> We, citizens of Israel who wish it to be a safe and thriving country, are worried by the continued political stalemate and by the occupation and settlements activities which lead to further confrontations with the Palestinians and torpedo the chances for a compromise. It is clear that the prospects for Israel's security and existence depend on the existence of a Palestinian state side by side with Israel. Israel should recognize the state of Palestine and Palestine should recognize the state of Israel, based on the June 4 1967 borders. Your initiative for recognising the state of Palestine will advance the prospects of peace and will encourage Israelis and Palestinians to bring an end to their conflict.

It is clear from my conversations that many Israeli citizens understand the deeply corrosive effect the occupation of Palestinian land, the apartheid system Israel has created and the brutal and dehumanising actions of the Israeli Defence Forces (IDF) are having on Israel.

One of those I spoke with – Yehuda Shaul – is a former sergeant and commander in the Israeli Army. He is co-director of 'Breaking the Silence', an organisation made up of former Israeli soldiers who speak out against the actions of the IDF, and is deeply concerned at the moral price Israel and its citizens are paying to maintain the occupation. He is also an Israeli patriot who believes that speaking out against injustice is necessary to defend Israel, as well as advance the rights of Palestinians.

Shaul dismisses Israeli government claims that its military operations are defensive and simply to oppose terrorism. He believes that that is only a small part of the strategy. 'It's all about offensive', he said, 'and maintaining Israeli military control over Palestinians.' He told me that the current Israeli policy of occupation and settlements is not designed as a temporary measure but is intended to be permanent. 'Occupation takes place every day; it is an offensive act every day.' He said it is a 'national security concept dependent on absolute control – a status quo that is not a frozen reality and is being entrenched every day'. He was clear in his conclusion also: 'The international community is failing Israelis and Palestinians. There is a lot of talk but no action. Nowhere in history', he said, 'did people wake up one morning and give up their privileges … the international community has to raise the price for Israel of the current status quo.' Shaul concluded: 'No one will live in dignity or freedom here, neither the Palestinians nor Israelis, until there is a sovereign Palestinian state. This is the right patriotic position.'

As I travelled across Israel and Palestine the landscape was full of walls. These were mostly small, dry stone walls to separate neighbours, or between farmland, or built to terrace fields on the side of rocky hills. But the separation wall is different. It is a scar on the land and conscience of Israel and of the international community. It stretches for 700 kilometres. It is multi-layered, often sixty metres wide in the exclusion zone with, in places, a concrete wall eight metres high.

It snakes up and down hills, alongside motorways, down the middle of streets and through Palestinian communities. It prevents Palestinian farmers from getting to their farmland. It captures within its boundary Palestinian land that is then annexed by the Israeli government. The separation wall, and the sterile roads that Palestinians are banned from, are symptomatic of an institutionalised, deliberately structured system of economic, cultural and social apartheid that brings shame to Israel and to the international community that has failed to take a stand against it.

The motion passed by the Dáil provides a route map for progress for the Irish government and for the international community. Last night Palestinian representatives who attended the Dáil debate were very uplifted by the outcome, so too were those Israeli activists whom I have kept in touch with in recent days. But all of us who support peace between Israelis and Palestinians know that there is a lot of hard work ahead before we achieve that historic conclusion.

Addendum

Three years later and the Irish government still refuse to abide by the Oireachtas vote and formally recognise the Palestinian State and its Mission in Dublin as an embassy.

Refugees:
The Road to Compassion

10 September 2015

There are some images that are seared into the collective consciousness of humanity. Most are traumatic. In my lifetime the screaming face of a naked young girl – Kim Phuc – badly burned from a napalm attack, running down a road in Vietnam as US troops looked on, is one. Fr Edward Daly frantically waving a bloodstained handkerchief as a group of frightened men pass British soldiers carrying the body of another who was shot during the British Paras' assault in Derry on Bloody Sunday is another. There is the image from Soweto in 1976, where school children take on the military might of the apartheid South African regime. There are also the four little babies, in blood-splattered white shrouds, lying in an ice-cream freezer in Gaza last summer. The rubble of the Shankill as dust-covered men and women desperately scramble through the debris trying to find survivors. We each have our own memories of these and other events. We remember where we were when we first saw them. We can still feel the emotional jolt, the sadness, the shock, mixed with anger, which often turned to outrage.

Sometimes an image lifts the spirit and rekindles our belief in humanity, whether it is ordinary citizens taking hammers and sledgehammers to the Berlin Wall, or the release of Nelson Mandela. Sometimes the image or piece of film is one that shocks and distresses. The public and personal reaction, however, is often short-lived as the next shocking image emerges onto our television screens or in our newspapers. They rarely have a lasting political impact. The image comes and goes. It remains in our memories. But the media move on to the next event and the political leaders and governments, having expressed their condemnation, put it behind them.

But there are exceptions.

The harrowing and distressing photo published on 2 September of three-year-old Aylan Kurdi lying on a beach in Turkey is one of these. How many times have you walked into a bedroom and looked into a cot, or onto a bed, and watched your son or daughter or grandchild lying peacefully asleep with their face pressed into the mattress and backside sticking up defiantly? But Aylan was not asleep. His death was not peaceful. He died with his five-year-old brother Galip and mother Rihan and seven other refugees trying to cross the five dangerous miles from Turkey – which is outside the EU – to the Greek island of Kos, which is inside the EU.[1]

In April 2015 as many as 700 men, women and children died when a boat carrying refugees sank about sixty miles off the coast of Libya. In response to this disaster and other incidents, in which boats sank and people drowned, the EU increased its naval presence in the region. The Irish government dispatched the *LÉ Eithne* in May. During its tour of duty it saved thousands. Lieutenant Commander Eric Timon said: 'The numbers of people fleeing Africa for whatever reason … casting themselves adrift on unseaworthy vessels in the hope of rescue or the hope of reaching European shores, it's quite extraordinary.'

The *LÉ Eithne* was replaced by *LÉ Niamh*. Together they have rescued an astounding 5,500 people to date. *LÉ Samuel Beckett*

---

1   Since this article was written it has been discovered that the deceased child from the picture was actually called Alan and his mother was Rehanna.

will shortly take over this essential humanitarian work. If the Irish boats hadn't been there all of those people might well have died. But despite the efforts of the Irish naval vessels and others from many countries the deaths are continuing. Last week, as the world mourned a little Syrian child and grieved with his father for the family he has lost, another 200 refugees drowned less than a mile off the Libyan coast. Some had been locked in the hold of the ship unable to escape. So far in 2015 over 2,500 have died in the Mediterranean sea.

But now the media and political focus has shifted. Thousands of desperate Syrians, Eritreans, Kurds and others have taken to the roads of Europe. They are walking hundreds of kilometres from Greece, up through the Balkans, to Germany. The Hungarian government has behaved shamefully but ordinary citizens along their route have demonstrated great compassion to this unfolding human tragedy.

It was into this crisis that the dreadful image of Aylan Kurdi injected a greater sense of political momentum. Germany has said it will take up to a million refugees. Other states have been less forthcoming as their governments enter into a new round of negotiations to discuss how they will respond to this crisis.

The cynic in me says that the more positive noises in recent days from European governments has less to do with the photo of a dead child on a beach and more to do with the countless thousands of refugees who are on the roads of Europe – no longer penned in camps or ports in Italy and Greece. This is a human catastrophe that can no longer be ignored or politically defused with a quota agreement that targets 40,000 when hundreds of thousands – millions – are on the move.

Martin McGuinness moved quickly to argue that the North should take several thousand refugees. The Irish government is still deciding what it should do, but it is difficult to see how it cannot agree to substantially increase the miserly 600 it was to take under the previous quota system. It needs to decide this quickly and to respond generously. Perhaps it's because we are an island people, colonised for centuries, who have been forced to flee in our millions for freedom and work, or perhaps it's because we naturally abhor injustice. But, whatever the reason, the public response has been amazing. Thousands of offers of accommodation and help, including collections of clothing, have been made. Ordinary citizens have opened their hearts and are pledging to open their homes also to help those in need.

The governments of Europe have a responsibility to do more. It was their greed and imperial ambitions that created the context for much of this crisis 100 years ago. It was the political and military decisions they have taken in the decades since, and mostly recently in respect of Palestine, Iraq, Syria, Libya and Afghanistan, that have shaped the violent maelstrom that is gripping the Middle East and north Africa. In Syria alone hundreds of thousands have died; seven million citizens have been forced from their homes and communities within the country and more than five million are scattered in refugee camps in surrounding states.

The conditions in the camps are appalling and are set to get worse. The United Nations humanitarian agencies have no money and cannot meet the needs of millions. In recent months food rations for Syrian refugees in Lebanon and Jordan, as well as in north Africa, have been cut. Many healthcare services run by the UN in Iraq have been closed. Last month 184 health clinics run by the World Health Organisation in Iraq were also closed. WHO needs $60 million for Iraq. Thus far it has only raised $5 million.

A recent report in the *Guardian* newspaper quoted one Syrian refugee, Fatmeh, who said of her two children in Lebanon: 'When we can't afford both medicine and food, I tie scarves around my boys' bellies at night so they don't wake up crying from stomach aches because they are hungry.'

Is it any wonder that families have chosen to make the perilous journey to Europe? It's time that the EU institutions, European governments and Mr Kenny and his colleagues, agreed to be as generous and as imaginative and as compassionate as this crisis demands of them.

Addendum

The first Irish naval vessel to be deployed to the Mediterranean to assist in the refugee operations was the *LÉ Eithne*. It was deployed on 16 May 2015. By June 2017 it and the *LÉ Niamh*, *LÉ Samuel Beckett*, *LÉ Róisín* and *LÉ James Joyce* had rescued over 15,600 migrants.

COLLUSION
AND LEGACY

Memories of 1969

For some people the most recent phase of conflict or 'the Troubles' in the North commenced in October 1968 when a civil rights march was attacked on Duke Street in Derry by the RUC. For others it was when the UVF carried out a series of bomb attacks on electricity lines and water pipelines in March and April 1969. But for many the Troubles began with the Battle of the Bogside in Derry in August 1969 and the attacks on the Catholic area of the Falls Road in west Belfast and the Ardoyne area of north Belfast that same month.

My memory of the Falls area at that time is very clear. Back then it was a multitude of small back-to-back red brick houses in row after row of narrow streets. Like many other parts of Belfast they had been constructed in the shadow of the linen mills and housed the workers who slaved under the worst of conditions for the most meagre of wages. Most of those who worked in the mills were women and children, mostly girls. They started work at 6.30 a.m. each morning and worked until 6 p.m. each evening. On Saturday they worked until noon. The quality of life was very bad. Wages were low, disease was widespread, the diet was very poor and the death rate was high.

The summer of 1969 was a very tense period. The unionist regime at Stormont was resisting any meaningful reforms. Ian Paisley was leading counter-demonstrations to civil rights marches. And several nationalists – Samuel Devenny in Derry, Francis McCloskey in Dungiven and Patrick Corry in Fermanagh – had already died as a result of injuries received in beatings from the RUC. Civil rights marches had been banned from town centres for over a year and beaten off the streets. But in Derry the Apprentice Boys, one of the unionist marching orders, were granted permission to march through the city centre and along the walls looking down into the Bogside, a predominately nationalist/Catholic part of the city.

At the edge of the Bogside young nationalists clashed with loyalists and the RUC launched baton charges. Fighting side by side with the loyalists, the RUC brought up armoured cars and – for the first time in Ireland – CS gas. For forty-eight hours the mainly teenage defenders of the Bogside used stones, bottles and petrol bombs against the constant baton charges of hundreds of RUC and loyalists. Exploiting high-rise flats to great effect, they lobbed petrol bombs at their attackers and succeeded in keeping them at bay.

In Belfast tension was at fever pitch. There was an emergency meeting of the Civil Rights Association on 13 August, which I attended, and from which came an appeal for solidarity demonstrations across the North against the events in Derry. I went from that meeting to one in Divis Flats, which I chaired. It was agreed we would march to the RUC barracks at Hasting Street and then to the RUC barracks on the Springfield Road. As we assembled in front of Divis Flats, our mood was defiant. We sang 'We Shall Overcome' amid chants of 'SS/RUC' and carried placards saying, 'The people of the Falls support the people of Derry.' The RUC attacked the march and this led to heavy rioting in Divis Street.

I remember leaving Springhill for the Falls on the late evening of 14 August. There the situation was one of bedlam. A loyalist mob, including many members of the B Specials armed with rifles, revolvers and sub-machine guns, had gathered on the Shankill Road and moved along the streets leading to the Falls. They petrol-bombed nationalist houses that lay on their route, beating up their occupants and shooting at fleeing residents. This loyalist mob invaded the Falls and, as it reached the Falls Road itself, started to attack St Comgall's school. The IRA opened fire and a loyalist gunman was killed. Now the RUC, coming in behind the loyalist civilians and B Specials, opened up with heavy-calibre Browning machine guns from Shorland armoured cars. They directed their firing into the narrow streets and into Divis flats itself, where they killed a nine-year-old boy, Patrick Rooney, and a young local man, Hugh McCabe, home on leave from the British Army.

Within a remarkably short space of time, the streets off the Falls Road, and the Falls itself, had been turned into a war zone. The IRA's armed intervention throughout Belfast was an extremely limited one. The real defence of the area was conducted by young people with petrol bombs and stones and bricks, though the IRA actions in the Falls and in Ardoyne were crucially important in halting the loyalist mobs at decisive times. However, Bombay Street, Dover Street and Percy Street were burned out and fighting continued all night in Conway Street. In Ardoyne scores of homes were attacked and many destroyed in Hooker Street and Brookfield Street.

As dawn arose on the morning of 15 August, it did so over a scene of absolute devastation. Six people were dead, five nationalists and one unionist; about 150 had been wounded by gunfire and hundreds of nationalist homes had been gutted. The unionist regime had also responded by introducing internment and twenty-four men from across the North had been arrested – all nationalists or republicans.

A pall of smoke rose over the Falls. The old familiar streetscape was shattered. The environment that I grew up in was gone. The self-contained, enclosed village atmosphere of the area and its peaceful sense of security had been brutally torn apart, leaving our close-knit community battered and bleeding. The everyday world in which we lived our childhood had been destroyed. None of us knew what it presaged for the years ahead. But we did know that things had changed utterly.

The Long Road to the Truth

17 June 2010

By 2.30 p.m. on 15 June 2010 the crowd at Free Derry corner had swollen and spread towards the Bloody Sunday memorial. The Bogside nestled below the city walls, basking in warm summer sunshine. Stewards shepherded members of the Bloody Sunday families and other relations of victims of state killings, like the Ballymurphy families, to the front of the mass of people. Eleven people – ten men, including a local priest, and a mother of eight children – were killed in Ballymurphy in west Belfast by the Parachute Regiment in the thirty-six hours following the introduction of internment in August 1971, six months before Bloody Sunday in Derry.

There was a good-natured sense of expectation as thousands of people fell in behind the families to complete the march that had ended in gunfire and death thirty-eight years earlier on 30 January 1972, the day known as Bloody Sunday. They were on their way to hear the outcome of the Saville Report into those events. The names of the fourteen victims of Bloody Sunday were read aloud. There was a minute's silence. Then we set off for the Guild Hall, the destination of the original civil rights march in 1972. As we passed Pilot's Row Community Centre someone started to sing 'We Shall Overcome' and I was swept back over forty years ago:

> The truth shall make us free, the truth shall make us free,
> The truth shall make us free someday;
> Oh, deep in my heart, I do believe
> The truth shall make us free someday.

In the Guild Hall Square the crowds cheered loudly as family members, ensconced inside the city chambers reading the Saville Report, waved copies of the report from the stained-glass windows and gave thumbs-up signals. We knew then, even before listening to the British Prime Minister speaking from the parliament in London and relayed live on a big screen, that the families felt vindicated. Today was their day. Today was a day for those killed and injured. Today was a day for those who campaigned for almost forty years for truth and justice. And when they trooped out of the Guild Hall they were greeted with a rapturous welcome. Tony Doherty, whose father was killed by the Paras, clearly expressed the families' feelings:

> The victims of Bloody Sunday have been vindicated. The Parachute Regiment has been disgraced. Widgery's great lie has been laid bare. The truth has been brought home at last. It can now be proclaimed to the world that the dead and the wounded of Bloody Sunday, civil rights marchers, were innocent one and all …
>
> The Parachute Regiment are the front line assassins for Britain's political and military elite. The report of the Saville Tribunal confirms this …
>
> … democracy itself … needs know what happened here on 30 January 1972. The British people need to know. The Irish people need to know. The world needs to know.
>
> Just as the civil rights movement of forty years ago was part of something huge happening all over the world, so the repression that came upon us was the same as is suffered by ordinary people everywhere who dare to stand up against injustice.
>
> Sharpville. Grozny. Tiananmen Square. Darfur. Fallujah. Gaza. Let our truth stand as their truth too.

Representatives of all the families spoke. One by one, they declared their relative, their brother, their father, their uncle, 'innocent!' Their remarks were interrupted by loud applause. People cried and cheered. And cheered and cried. Clenched fists stabbed the air. Not the clenched fists of young radicals. These were elderly Derry grannies and grandas. Elderly widows. Middle-aged siblings.

Today was their day. There was an air of celebration. Of achievement. Of pride. Of release. At the end one of the women relatives tore up a copy of the Widgery Report – a report which had been part of the British state's initial cover-up of what happened, a lie it stuck to for decades – and flung it to the wind. I picked up some of the pieces afterwards and placed them in my copy of Saville, a keepsake of a remarkable day.

On the way home someone had placed hundreds of little name plaques along the grass verge at the side of the road outside Dungiven, Co. Derry. The names were of hundreds of citizens killed by the British Army and other state forces here during the conflict, including the eleven from Ballymurphy. Mr Cameron should know they and their families continue to be denied truth. His apology for Bloody Sunday was right. But he said that 'Bloody Sunday is not the defining story of the service the British Army gave in Northern Ireland from 1969–2007.'

That is wrong. Bloody Sunday *is* the defining story of the British Army in Ireland.

The Dublin and Monaghan Bombs and the British Government

20 April 2011

I questioned Taoiseach Enda Kenny about his meeting on Monday with the British Prime Minister and asked him whether he had raised the Dublin and Monaghan bombings in which thirty-four Irish citizens were killed and hundreds more injured? Specifically, I asked the Taoiseach if he had raised directly with the British Prime Minister the Dáil request from July 2008 for the British government to hand over all files and other information in relation to the bomb attacks on 17 May 1974 and other atrocities inquired into by Justice Barron, and for these files to be opened to independent, international scrutiny.

The Taoiseach was evasive in his response. But the only conclusion to be drawn from what he said is that he didn't. This failure to act in Irish national interests or in the interests of Irish citizens is characteristic of the submissive attitude of Irish governments to British governments over the years. The colonisation and occupation of Ireland over many centuries by Britain has left a bitter legacy. Part of this is an inability on the part of Irish governments to stand up for Irish interests when dealing with British governments.

The Taoiseach described the relationship between the two states as one based on mutual respect and trust. How much respect has a British government for an Irish government and for Ireland when it hides the truth of its involvement in collusion and murder, and refuses to hand over vital information on this issue? How much self-respect does an Irish government have if it refuses to challenge that British government on this important issue?

The citizens who died in the Dublin and Monaghan bombings were not the first to die as a result of collusion, nor the last. In 2006 an Independent International Panel on Alleged Collusion in Sectarian Killings produced a detailed 109-page report into the activities of the Glenanne Gang. The gang's name derived from a farm at Glenanne, near Markethill in Co. Armagh, from which it carried out many of its attacks. It followed a careful examination of twenty-five cases of unionist paramilitary violence between 1972 and 1977 in which seventy-six people were killed. The panel found that in twenty-four cases involving seventy-four killings there was evidence of RUC and Ulster Defence Regiment (UDR) collusion. This included the Dublin and Monaghan bombs and the bomb attack in December 1975 in which two Dundalk men, Jack Rooney and Hugh Watters, were killed.

The report revealed that the British government knew of the collusion between the RUC, British Army and unionist death squads as far back as the early 1970s. Sometimes official state forces donned masks and carried out the killings themselves. At other times they simply passed the weaponry, know-how and information on to surrogate unionist paramilitaries.

Launching the report in 2006, Douglass Cassel, a human rights professor from the American University of Notre Dame, said he had been shocked at the extent of state collusion in the killings the team had investigated. The panel had found evidence of collusion with British state forces, primarily the RUC and UDR, in twenty-four of the twenty-five cases they examined. In most cases the evidence was extremely strong. In some cases they concluded that there was 'a prima facie case', that is sufficient evidence to warrant a prosecution.

After the killings came the cover-up. It involved state forces covering up their own crimes and the crimes of others, hiding weaponry, failing to pursue investigations and refusing to prosecute despite overwhelming evidence. In one case, Robin Jackson – a notorious unionist gunman – was identified by the widow of one of his victims, but the charges against him were subsequently dropped by order of the Director of Public Prosecutions (DPP). Jackson was later exposed as a Special Branch agent.

The cases investigated included car bombings, grenade attacks and shootings, including mass killings, as in the Miami Showband attack on 31 July 1975, when three members of the popular showband were killed by the Ulster Volunteer Force (UVF) as they were returning to Dublin after a performance in Banbridge, Co. Down.

In addition to the activities of the loyalist Glenanne Gang, British agents like Brian Nelson helped procure weapons through apartheid South African connections in 1988. These weapons were secured for the use of three unionist paramilitary organisations: the Ulster Defence Association (UDA), UVF and Ulster Resistance. The first two have, according to the Independent International Commission on Decommissioning, since gotten rid of their weapons. Ulster Resistance has not.

The importation of these weapons with the help of British intelligence led to a dramatic increase in murders by unionist death squads. In the six years before the arrival of the South African weapons, from January 1982 to December 1987, unionist murder gangs killed seventy-one people. In the six years after the arrival of the arms shipment that number climbed to 229. The unionist death squads were assisted in all of this by RUC Special Branch and British agencies like Force Research Unit (FRU), British Military Intelligence and the British Security Services. Among those murdered was human rights lawyer, Pat Finucane. Special

Branch agents and British intelligence agents were involved in his murder, including providing the information, the weapons, giving the order and even in carrying out the murder.

Over the decades of conflict, thousands of files and photos of nationalists and republicans were passed over to unionist death squads, commonly from within the UDR, and frequently proper investigations of sectarian murders were not carried out by the RUC.

In 2001 a Commission of Inquiry under Mr Justice Henry Barron was established by the Irish government. Four reports were published and a sub-committee of the cross-party Joint Oireachtas Committee on Justice, Equality, Defence and Women's Rights conducted an extensive examination of the reports. The sub-committee concluded 'that given that we are dealing with acts of international terrorism that were colluded in by the British security forces, the British Government cannot legitimately refuse to co-operate with investigations and attempts to get to the truth'.

Despite this hard-hitting conclusion, and the mountain of evidence available, no Irish government has pursued this issue vigorously. Enda Kenny promised a different kind of government from that of Fianna Fáil, but if his meeting in Downing Street is an example of how he does business, it would appear to be the same old story.

The Tiger Hunt Mindset and Shoot-to-Kill

20 March 2012

The role of British forces in countless actions overseas after the Second World War were generally presented publicly as 'policing actions'. The enemy was often presented as a criminal or a terrorist or a communist, and propaganda served up by a largely compliant British media presented the 'enemy' as sub-human, subversive, cruel, ruthless and brutal. In truth, these military operations were desperate attempts by a dying imperial power to hang on to colonies that were demanding independence.

By the time of Operation Banner – the British Army name for its military involvement in the North from 1969 – the British Empire was part of history. It had fought and lost in countless political and military actions in Africa, the Middle East, India and South-East Asia. This colonial experience of war and politics was a fundamental part of the British military psyche. It generated several theoretical books on the role of counter-insurgency techniques, with the most widely read, and the most influential, being Kitson's *Low Intensity Operations: Subversion, Insurgency and Counter-Insurgency*. In his book *War of the Flea* Robert Taber had argued that for a guerrilla movement to succeed it needed the support of the people or at the very least a significant proportion of the people. Kitson understood this, so his strategies were about subverting that support through reshaping government structures, the judiciary, the law, the police and the media, all with the aim of defeating the enemy. He wrote: 'The fundamental concept is the working of the triumvirate, civil, military and police, as a joint and integrated organisation from the highest to the lowest level of policy making, planning and administration.'

Kitson also defended the use of death squads and the corruption of the judicial process. Counter-gangs, which he formed and participated in while in Kenya, had been successful in helping defeat what was labelled as the 'Mau Mau insurgency' (although Britain still had to lower the flag and leave in 1964). Kitson wrote:

> Everything done by a government and its agents in combating insurgency must be legitimate. But this does not mean that the government must work within exactly the same set of laws during an emergency as existed beforehand. The law should be used as just another weapon in the government's arsenal, in which case it becomes little more than a propaganda cover for the disposal of unwanted members of the public.[1]

Kitson's writings, based on his experiences in Kenya, Malaya, Aden (in Yemen) and elsewhere, became standard practice for British operational procedures in the North, especially after he was appointed British Army commander in Belfast in the summer of 1970. Hiding behind the legitimacy of a law, which its government moulded to fit its objectives, the British Army embarked on a range of covert and overt actions, tactics and strategies which were about defeating the IRA.

The British military and political establishment's only interest in the violence of unionist death squads was in how effectively the UDA, the Red Hand Commando, the UVF and other loyalist groups could be used as counter-gangs against those the British

---

1   F. Kitson, *Gangs and Counter-Gangs* (Barrie and Rockcliffe, London, 1960), p. 46.

regarded as the real enemy – the republicans. Structured formal and informal collusion between elements of the British military and intelligence agencies and organisations became part of the British government's counter-insurgency strategy in Ireland, as did shoot-to-kill operations by British units and the RUC, the use of plastic bullets as a means of community control, torture and ill-treatment of prisoners, special courts and special rules in the courts and much more.

Recently, some new material has become available through the British government's state records office which highlights the British military's approach to Ireland. In June 1989 Lieutenant General Sir John Waters, who was then the general officer commanding (GOC) in the North, wrote a lengthy detailed proposal to the officer commanding, Armoured Infantry Training and Advisory Team about the preparation work that new British Army units about to be deployed in the North needed to undertake. His 'Concept of Operations' paper is interesting because of the insight it gives into the mindset of the general running the British Army in the North at the time. Waters wrote:

> It is well established that the terrorists and their supporters use a mass of fabricated complaints against the Security Forces as a means of trying to discredit them and increase their alienation from the nationalist community … Some inconvenience – delays as a result of checkpoints and collateral damage during searches etc. – is inescapable in any counter-insurgency operation. However we must recognise that if in the past and still today there were not some cases of real stupidity or wilful rudeness or careless damage by policemen and soldiers, the terrorists would have little prospect of success for their allegations of widespread insensitive behaviour.
>
> I have looked very carefully into the whole matter of complaints. I entirely accept that the number of cases in which soldiers

offend, almost invariably under some sort of provocation, is in the circumstances amazingly low. Nevertheless in the context of what has gone before in the Province and the heightened sensitivities that have resulted each 'offence' is one too many and entirely unhelpful. Incidents which anywhere else would be seen as an innocent soldier's prank or just an expression of youthful high spirits can give real offence.

Later in a section under 'Discipline and Propaganda' Waters wrote: 'Most of what they say about bad behaviour by soldiers is lies. But it is believed by many, particularly in the nationalist community.'

So there you have it. The truth according to Waters is that nationalists and many others around the world were all gullible. The thousands of wrecked homes, the communities oppressed by occupying British troops, the deaths of almost 400 people in disputed circumstances and over a thousand more in attacks by loyalist counter-gangs, the beatings and the terror were all just 'youthful high spirits' or the result of 'some sort of provocation' or a prank!

But Waters' denial of reality doesn't just stop there. He describes how the RUC and the British Army consist of 'standard units' and 'specialist units (Special Forces)'. He wrote: 'In very general terms the "standard units" provide the constant presence on the ground to give Reassurance and Deterrence. Attrition operations are usually carried out by the specialist units – but not always.'

And then the colonial mindset kicked in. The years of Britain being a colonial overlord in colonies across the globe found voice. Waters reduces the killing and capture of the enemy to a tiger hunt:

The way that the standard units and the specialist units should work together to get success can be compared with an old-fashioned tiger hunt. The most experienced hunters are placed in what is judged to be the very best position from which to get a shot. These are the specialist units. The beaters surround the area of the jungle where the tigers are expected to be and drive them on to the guns. These are the standard units. Beating requires great skill and co-ordination to prevent the tigers breaking out of the cordon, of killing some of the beaters. Frequently the tigers break back, make a mistake and expose themselves to the beaters. This is the opportunity for the beaters, who also carry guns, to get a tiger.

And there you have it – 'the disposal of unwanted members of the public' as Kitson called it.[2] Shoot-to-kill operations were modelled on 'tiger hunts'!

Is it any wonder that two months later Waters' boss, Major General Guthrie, who was assistant chief of the general staff, wrote to him asking that he reword his paper? Guthrie admitted to 'brooding and re-reading your tiger shoot letter' following a visit to Waters in the North. While he regarded the paper as excellent, Guthrie was worried that the use of the 'tiger hunt' example would get out sooner or later and cause 'you and the Army department and Ministers' embarrassment. He added: 'I am convinced that you are running an unnecessary risk and you would achieve your aim – which I fully understand and applaud – just as well in another way.'

Waters was having none of it and told him no. He refused to temper his language and stuck to his guns – pardon the pun. There is a danger in reading Waters' language that you almost dismiss him as a pompous, jingoistic Colonel Blimp-like character, but he was the general in charge of the British Army in the North. He and those who held that post before him, and others in a host

---

2   Kitson, *Gangs and Counter-Gangs*, p. 46.

of intelligence, policing and military agencies, took decisions that had a profound impact on the lives of citizens in the North. And it is clear from Guthrie's letter that he was not dissenting from the sentiment, just the use of language.

It is no accident that those places which were the target of such tactics and strategies remain conflict zones to this day. The one significant exception is Ireland and that has been achieved despite our military overlords and colonial tiger hunters.

For that we give thanks.

A State in Denial

1 November 2016

As I have already discussed in previous articles, in October 2016 the British government revealed plans to opt out of the European Convention on Human Rights. Prime Minister May set it in the context of trying to end what she called the 'industry of vexatious claims' against British soldiers in Iraq and in Afghanistan – those she described as the 'finest armed forces known to man'. The real purpose is to protect British soldiers from the legal consequences of breaking international human rights law.

But there is a deeper, more self-centred motive for the actions of the British political establishment – it is about protecting itself. If we have learned anything in the decades of conflict in the North and since, it is that the security apparatus of the British state – its soldiers, police and intelligence agencies – only operates according to rules and regulations laid down by the government. In order to defend these, and those political leaders who create the legal and strategic framework within which they operate, the state has to ensure that the political establishment is protected.

In this respect successive British governments, both Conservative and Labour, have been very successful. How could they not be? British governments create and fund the organisations that are responsible for investigating any illegality. They pass the laws that define the powers and limitations of investigations. And as in the current row over money for legacy inquests, they can deny investigators and the families of victims access to information and to the funding needed to carry out those investigations.

An example of this came in February 2016 after the North's

Lord Chief Justice Sir Declan Morgan proposed a blueprint to deal with all outstanding inquests – some are over forty years old – which would cost ten million pounds. The plan would cover ninety-seven deaths linked to the conflict. A further eighty-seven are being considered for inquest. The British government is so far refusing to release the money.

However, the tenacity of families and of those who support them and the nature of the huge bureaucracy that is needed to run a modern political system means that sometimes the veil is lifted and the extent of political and security corruption is revealed.

Margaret Urwin's *A State in Denial* (Mercier Press, 2016) is a case in point. Through meticulous research and by combing through huge volumes of British state papers Margaret succeeds in uncovering a murky and duplicitous world in which the British state sanctions murder and then engages in a political and propaganda strategy to deny it. In one sense much of what is written about in *A State in Denial* is not new. We have known for decades that the British government used the colonial tactics of counter-insurgency and of counter-gangs to create the UDA, and then facilitated the actions of that organisation and of the UVF. Collusion was a matter of institutional and administrative practice. The murder of human rights lawyer Pat Finucane by agents of the British state, using information provided by that state, is one example of this. But there are countless others.

A State in Denial provides overwhelming evidence for this by relying on the words of British civil servants, politicians and soldiers. In countless declassified documents, dated and detailed, the depth of collusion between the British government and its military, policing and judicial system is exposed, and the lengths to which that government will go to lie about all of this is laid bare for all to read.

This is especially true of the British government's attitude to the UDA, which it refused to ban for twenty years despite a huge volume of evidence of its involvement in sectarian killings. Following its creation the UDA was used as an extension of the British state's security apparatus. In one document dated October 1971, shortly after internment was introduced, it was decided to allow loyalist 'vigilantes' to work with the British Army. In orders from the British commander of land forces, British Army units were told to:

> effect informal contact with unofficial forces in order that the activities and areas of operation can be co-ordinated and taken in account in the security plans for the areas concerned. The aim will be to effect liaison normally at company or platoon level between the security forces and all unofficial bodies who are seen to be working in the public interest.

As Margaret Urwin concludes:

> All of the evidence from these official documents suggests that by the end of 1971 loyalist paramilitaries were in a favoured position ... shielded from internment ... and a decision was taken by the army and the British and Northern Ireland governments to adopt loyalists as an auxiliary force.

This approach extended to British ministers publicly claiming that the UDA was little more than an ad hoc group of individuals and poorly organised vigilante groups. However, in a letter sent on 10 July 1972 a senior civil servant tells the cabinet secretary that 'these groups are now well-disciplined, centrally co-ordinated'.

The British state bias toward loyalists and especially the UDA, and the role of the locally recruited UDR, is revealed in an internal British Army memo of 31 July 1972:

The UDA is not an illegal organisation and membership of the UDA is not an offence under the military laws; it is also a large organisation not all of whose members can be regarded as dangerous extremists. One important (but unspoken) function of the UDR is to channel into a constructive and disciplined direction Protestant energies which might otherwise become disruptive. For these reasons it is felt that it would be counter-productive to discharge a UDR member on the grounds that he was a member of the UDA.

The UDR was established in 1970. It was a locally recruited regiment of the British Army. Its purpose was to replace the B Specials – an infamous auxiliary state police force that was almost entirely unionist. Hundreds of UDR soldiers were imprisoned over the years for their part in loyalist paramilitary activities. It was effectively disbanded in 1992 and merged into the Royal Irish Regiment.

The approach towards the UDA outlined in the army memo facilitated the arming of that organisation. In a document entitled 'Subversion in the UDR', which is dated August 1973 and written by the British Army Military Intelligence and Psychological Operations staff, it is noted that 'joint membership of the UDA and the UDR became widespread and at the same time the rate of UDR weapons losses greatly increased'. These 'losses' went to the UDA and the UVF.

Margaret Urwin quotes from a Historical Enquiries Team (HET) report which states that 'between October 1970 and March 1973, 222 weapons – including thirty-two handguns – belonging to the UDR were misplaced, lost or stolen from the homes of soldiers, UDR armouries, duty posts, or while in transit'.

At the same time British ministers were denying that the UDA was involved in sectarian killings. In evidence to the European

Commission on Human Rights in February 1975 General Tuzo, a former GOC for the North, and former RUC Chief Constable Robert Shillington both denied that the UDA was engaged in a campaign of terror. Tuzo said: 'The UDA was not a terrorist organisation ... not a terrorist campaign. I would not describe it as terrorist at all, but this does not preclude at all, of course, the campaign of murders and things later on, but that cannot necessarily be levelled at the UDA.'

Shillington was even more direct: 'The UDA declare themselves, they state who they are, there is no evidence that they engaged systematically in campaigns of terrorism.'

The reality was very different. Between April and December 1972 loyalist groups killed 101 people; 63 were killed by the UDA. Despite this, British Labour and Conservative governments defended the claim that the UDA was not banned because it did not carry out sectarian assassinations. In private their position was very different. An internal British briefing paper, 'A Guide to Paramilitary and Associated Organisations' dated 2 September 1976 describes the UDA as:

> the largest and best-organised of the Loyalist paramilitary organisations. It tries to maintain a respectable front and, to this end, either denies responsibility for sectarian murders and terrorist bombings or claims them in the name of the Ulster Freedom Fighters (UFF), a proscribed and essential fictitious organisation which is widely known to be a nom de guerre for the UDA.

Margaret Urwin's book adds significantly to our understanding of the decades of conflict and in particular the British government's central role in perpetuating it. During those years, and since, the British government has dismissed or ignored the concerns raised by individuals and organisations, including the Irish government, surrounding its knowledge of and role in collusion. How often have Irish governments been rebutted when they have asked the British government about the Dublin and Monaghan bombs? Do British governments care that within days of those attacks they legalised the very organisation that, along with its double agents, was responsible for them?

Margaret Urwin's *A State in Denial* precisely describes the attitude of the British government today. But that denial is not a result of some misplaced sense of loyalty to those state agencies and political leaders that directed and carried out collusion. It is a product of the underlying imperial mindset that ordered ruthless wars on citizens in Kenya, Malaya, Aden, Cyprus and the North, and engaged in countless other colonial wars, including in Afghanistan and Iraq. It's the mindset that believes that the British Empire was decent and good and benign, a mindset that was exploited successfully in the immigration arguments heard during the Brexit campaign.

MOVING
SOUTH

Not Going Away,
You Know

16 November 2010

'You're mad!' RG said.

'What do you mean I'm mad?'

'Going to Louth – abandoning the people of west Belfast. It'll all end in tears.'

'Well,' I said, 'when you talk the talk you also have to walk the walk. The country's in a mess. People are crying out for leadership and a way to regain our sense of ourselves.'

'And you think you can do something about that? Who's going to represent west Belfast?'

'The people will sort that out. And I'm not leaving west Belfast. I'm standing down from my public responsibilities here. But this is where I live. It's where Colette and our family live. It's my community. It's where my church is, my GAA club, my county.'

'So, you think you're going to get elected in Louth?'

'Well, that's the intention. There's no guarantees. Wee Arthur [Arthur Morgan was the sitting Sinn Féin TD for Louth] is a hard act to follow. And it is a challenge. Look, Sinn Féin is the only all-island party. There are two different sets of policy positions, currencies and political establishments because of partition. But the problems are the same. I'm two or three days in the South every week, as you know. And sometimes two or three days in the Assembly. So, it's hard to do both to the extent that is required.'

'And what about the peace process?' he asked.

'Martin and I work very closely together and we don't take

the peace process for granted. I'll continue to work on that. But you have seen people coming up to me in distress at what the government in Dublin is doing. And Fine Gael and Labour have bought into that agenda. We are the only ones proposing a better way forward. I'm one of the people calling on citizens to make a stand. So I've decided to make a stand myself and, by the way, all the work I do on suicide prevention, on justice issues like the Ballymurphy and Springhill Massacres, I'll be able to bring them to a different platform.'

'If you get elected!'

RG was really in a tizzy. 'I know this idea has been kicked about for nine or ten years now,' he exclaimed, 'but why now? What about the regeneration projects in west Belfast?'

'We're going to push ahead with those. Look, I know this is a big thing. I had to decide personally whether I was up for it. Whether I wanted to put my family through another roller-coaster ride. Whether I could wrench myself away from the work that I do here in the west of the city. And when I did eventually come round to the conclusion that I would be prepared to take this initiative, apart from Colette, the first people I spoke to were the Belfast and west Belfast leaderships of Sinn Féin. And then our leadership in Co. Louth. We had lengthy discussions and we're all at one on this. A struggle is about taking risks. It's about acting in the common good. Our struggle at its essence is about Ireland and the people of Ireland. So, there you are,' I concluded.

'You don't have to give me all that bullshit. Who's going to thank you for this?'

'I'm not looking for thanks.'

'You're looking to get your head chopped off. You're handing it to the Staters on a plate. The establishment is going to come at you – like a tornado.'

I decided to provoke him.

'Did you ever read Robert Frost?' I asked. 'Two roads diverged in a wood … I took the one less travelled by … And that has made all the difference.'

He looked at me with a smirk. 'You're full of it!' he exclaimed. 'And,' he said coyly with a little smile, 'you're leaving me.'

'No I'm not,' I said. 'You're coming with me.'

'Seriously?'

'Yep!'

'Well I'm up for that! The only thing is,' he hesitated, 'I feel like Che Guevara before he went to Bolivia.'

'We'll be all right,' I said.

'I suppose so,' he said. 'Let's do it. Up the Republic!'

'Now who is full of it?' I asked him.

'Well,' he replied, 'we're not going away, you know. Just down the road a wee bit. Up Louth.'

'Turncoat,' I said, '*Aontroim Abú*! Up Antrim!'

A New Type of Politics

14 December 2010

I am the Sinn Féin candidate for Louth and East Meath. In the Fairways Hotel party activists from across the constituency unanimously and enthusiastically endorsed my candidacy. I thank them for that. Louth, like all the border counties, has suffered grievously because of partition. The Good Friday Agreement has provided a peaceful and democratic way to unite the Irish people. Sinn Féin is committed to this. The general election, when it comes, will be the most important in recent decades. There is huge public dissatisfaction and anger at the revelations of corruption within the political system. There is frustration and resentment at the policies of parties whose goal is to bail out the banks and their developer friends in the golden circle, while handing over sovereignty to the International Monetary Fund (IMF) and the EU.

I believe that citizens are looking for a new kind of politics. A type of politics that they can trust, that empowers and includes them. A politics that sets aside elites, doesn't pander to the wealthy and seeks to build a new kind of Ireland. There is no more important or relevant time than this for republican politics and core republican values. Take down the Proclamation of the Republic. Read it, carefully. It is about freedom and empowerment of citizens, and equality and inclusivity and sovereignty. It is about the nation – the whole nation – all thirty-two counties. It is about nation building.

So, how do we translate all of this into a new type of politics? How do we make genuine republicanism relevant for citizens?

Pearse Doherty, Sinn Féin's spokesperson on finance, spelled it out eloquently and passionately in his budget speech. It is about defending public services, constructing a new and fairer tax system, protecting the disabled and disadvantaged, as well as low and middle-income earners. It has to be about stimulating the economy and protecting and creating jobs, as well as promoting the interests of our rural communities, including the promotion of the farming community and fishing industry. There is also a need for a root and branch reform of this discredited political system.

Change is possible. Look at the peace process, imperfect though it is. Much more needs to be done by the Dáil to transcend partition and to have a single island policy focus. Good inclusive relationships need to be continuously fostered with unionists.

The gap between the political classes and the people needs to be removed. Politicians should be public servants. People are citizens. Citizens have the right to be involved in all matters of public policy. And politicians and other public servants must be accountable to their peers. All of this is an argument for republican systems of government; that is, systems in which the people are sovereign and equal.

Such a society has to be tolerant. Society must reflect and include the entirety of its people, not part of them. Why should gender or sexual orientation be the basis for the exclusion of anyone? Or disability? Why should race or class or skin colour or creed give one group of human beings the ability to deny other human beings their full rights or entitlements as citizens? And if citizens have rights, why are they not all-encompassing rights? Should the right to the basics for life not include economic rights as well as political and social?

I believe that all human beings have the right, as a birthright, to be treated equally. To have the right to a job, to a home, to equal access to a health service that is free at the point of delivery, to equal access to education at all levels for all our children and to a safe and clean environment. A rights-based society – a true republic – requires citizens to fulfil their obligations for the common good. It also requires the state to inform all citizens of their rights, and to uphold and defend those rights.

The political system in the twenty-six counties needs to be completely overhauled and democratised, and all with an eye to advancing the all-Ireland institutions and structures that will benefit society on this island. Historically, Ireland is a highly centralised society in its political administration, going back to the days when Britain ran the whole island from Dublin. Dublin has become more dominant still as a result of urbanisation and the shift in population from rural Ireland to the capital.

The Oireachtas needs radical reform, including a reform of the electoral system. Ministers should be more accountable and be paid significantly less. There should also be greater decentralisation, including the devolving of real powers to local communities in respect of schools, social care for the elderly and dependent, and improving the physical environment. Referendums could have a key place in politics, allowing the people themselves to legislate directly.

These are just some thoughts, some ideas of the new type of politics – republican politics – that might shape the future. And part of this means reaching out to others of a like mind, other progressive members of society who are prepared to build an alliance for a new Ireland and a new type of politics that is free of corruption and characterised by civic virtue and social justice.

In all of this we should be guided by Wolfe Tone's motto, which remains perennially relevant: to seek to politically unite all patriotic people 'under the common name of Irishman', which of course includes Irishwomen as well. There will be three elections in 2011. On 5 May – the thirtieth anniversary of Bobby Sands' death – the electorate in the North will vote in local government and Assembly elections. When the Taoiseach eventually calls an election, we will vote for a new Dáil. It looks like being an interesting year.

Addendum

The election in the South was held on 25 February 2011. Sinn Féin won fourteen seats, an increase of ten. In the 2016 election the party won an additional nine seats in the Dáil, bringing our total to twenty-three. We also increased our number of members of the Seanad from three to seven.

Politics can be a Funny Old Game

29 January 2011

Politics can be a funny old game. You never know from one day to the next what might turn up. But some days are even wackier than most. After the Taoiseach announced on 20 January 2011 that an election would take place on 11 March, I sat at a desk in the new Sinn Féin campaign office in Dundalk and scribbled a short handwritten note to John Bercow, the speaker of the British parliament:

> *A chara*, I hereby resign as MP for the constituency of west Belfast. *Go raibh maith agat.* Gerry Adams

This was in keeping with my commitment to the people of Louth and East Meath that when the election was called I would resign the West Belfast seat as a demonstration of my resolve to give that constituency 100 per cent. That was that.[1]

Meetings and more meetings and a plan for later in the day to visit a pharmaceutical conference in the Institute of Technology in Dundalk. And then David Cameron stood up in the British House of Commons and the schedule went out the window. He was being baited by Nigel Dodds of the DUP. Nigel made

---

1 Although Taoiseach Brian Cowen originally announced that the election would be on 11 March, the Green Party subsequently withdrew from the coalition government on 23 January, resulting in the election actually being held on 25 February.

me smile when he asked Cameron was he aware that 'one of the Members elected to this House has decided to emigrate'. The British Prime Minister then told his audience that I had agreed to accept an 'office of profit under the crown' by taking up the position of Crown Steward and Bailiff of the Manor of Northstead.[2] What had up to then been a rather boring news day for the media suddenly took on a new dimension. I should have known something was up when RG genuflected before me.

'Sire,' he said, 'methinks I should assemble the peasants in your honour.' I ignored him but then the phones started buzzing as the media wanted to know was it true? Had I suddenly become a feudal baron? Would they now have to tug the forelock and bend the knee when meeting me?

The fact is Mr Cameron's claim was untrue. I had simply resigned. There was no other contact with the Brits on any of this. There was no consultation and no one in the British system had asked would I even be remotely interested in taking up such an offer. Perhaps they already knew what my answer would be!

So, instead of asking for my opinion, the British Chancellor of the Exchequer decided to presume that my resignation was a request for such an office. The Brits frequently presume that they know what's best for others without asking first, hence their invasion of Iraq, their presence in Afghanistan and of course their occupation of this island.

I have been an Irish republican all my adult life and I have refused to have any truck whatsoever with these antiquated and quite bizarre aspects of the British parliamentary system. The

---

2   There is no mechanism in the British parliament to simply resign. A resolution was passed in 1624 to get around this. The resolution stated that those who resigned had to accept a 'paid office of the crown' – in this case the position of Crown Steward and Bailiff of the Manor of Northstead. This was done on the assumption that the newly titled member could not then criticise the government.

burghers of the manor of Northstead must have been as bemused as RG and I at this strange turn of events. He was now behaving like Baldrick out of *Blackadder*. Meantime I contacted Downing Street to demand to know what was going on. There were several conversations with David Cameron's private secretary and he apologised for what had happened. While I respect the right of British parliamentarians to have their own protocols and systems, no matter how odd these may appear to the rest of the world in general and Irish people in particular, the Prime Minister should not make claims which are untrue and inaccurate. I am proud to have represented the people of west Belfast for almost three decades and to have done so without pledging allegiance to the English Queen or accepting British parliamentary claims to jurisdiction in my country.

My first election contest was in west Belfast in 1982 for the Assembly elections. And from then until last week, with a short break in between, it has been an honour for me to represent the people of that fine constituency. I felt a real wrench as I posted my letter of resignation. I am very grateful to all those citizens who worked and voted for Sinn Féin through good times and bad times in defiance of the British government and its allies in Ireland. The onus is now on the Westminster parties to call a by-election as soon as possible in the west Belfast constituency. In the meantime let me assure the people of west Belfast that the Sinn Féin party will continue to provide our first-class constituency service and representation.

Candidatitis and Other Ailments

19 May 2014

At some point in any election campaign every candidate forms a view that they are going to win. This syndrome, which is known as candidatitis, is capable of moving even the most rational aspirant into a state of extreme self-belief. It strikes without warning, is no respecter of gender and can infect the lowly municipal hopeful as well as the lofty presidential wannabe.

Screaming Lord Sutch, or his Irish equivalent – who stand just for the craic – can fall victim to candidatitis as much as the most committed and earnest political activist. I believe this is due to two factors. First of all most people standing for election see little point in telling the voters that they are not going to win. That just wouldn't make sense. Of course not. So they say they are going to win.

Listen to Michael Howard, the British Tory leader. He had no chance of beating Blair's Labour Party in the 2005 general election. Did he admit that? Not on your nelly. Or, closer to home, listen to David Ford, the Alliance Party leader in the North. No chance of winning even half a seat in the current contest (held on 22 May 2014) but Ford sounds as confident as George W. Bush addressing an election rally in his native Texas.

That's when candidatitis starts. As the 'we are going to win' is repeated time and time again it starts to have a hypnotic effect on the person intoning the mantra. By this time it's too late. Which brings me to the second factor. Most people unintentionally encourage candidatitis. Not even the candidate's best friend will say, 'Hold on, you haven't a chance.' Except for the media. But no candidate believes the media. And most candidates are never interviewed by the media anyway.

So a victim of candidatitis will take succour from any friendly word from any punter. Even a 'good luck' takes on new meaning and 'I won't forget ye' is akin to a full-blooded endorsement. So are we to pity sufferers of this ailment? Probably not. They are mostly consenting adults, though in most elections many parties will run conscripts. In the main, these are staunch party people who are persuaded to run by more sinister elements who play on their loyalty and commitment.

In some cases these reluctant candidates run on the understanding that they are not going to get elected. Their intervention, they are told, is to stop the vote going elsewhere or to maintain the party's representative share of the vote. In some cases this works. But in other cases, despite everything, our reluctant hero, or heroine, actually gets elected. A friend of mine was condemned to years on the Belfast City Council years ago when his election campaign went horribly wrong. He topped the poll.

That's another problem. Topping the poll is a must for some of these candidates. Such ambition creates a headache for party managers. If the aim is to get a panel of party representatives elected, they all have to come in fairly evenly. This requires meticulous negotiation to carve up constituencies.

Implementing such arrangements makes the implementation of the Good Friday Agreement look easy. It requires an inordinate amount of discipline on the candidates' behalf. Most have this. Some don't. Some get really sneaky, particularly as the day of reckoning comes closer. Hot flushes and an allergy to losing can lead to some sufferers poaching a colleague's votes. This is a very painful condition leading to serious outbreaks of nastiness and reprisals and recriminations if detected before polling day. It usually cannot be treated and can have long-term effects.

So all of this is by way of lifting the veil on these usually unreported problems which infect our election contests. Politicians are a much maligned species. In some cases not without cause. Readers, if fully informed of the viruses caused by candidatitis, might be persuaded to take a more tolerant and benign view of the sometimes strange behaviour of those citizens who contest elections.

Love us or hate us, you usually get the politicians you deserve. Granted this might not always extend to governments, given the coalitions which come together in blatant contradiction of all election promises and commitments. The lust for power causes this. This condition is probably the most serious ailment affecting our political system and those who live there. It is sometimes terminal. But this comes after elections and is worthy of a separate study.

Before they get to that point, if they ever do, candidates suffer many torments. Space restrictions prevent me from documenting them all. So, don't ignore the visages on the multitudes of posters which defile lamp posts and telegraph poles during election times, and in some cases for years afterwards. Think of the torment that poor soul is suffering. When you are accosted by a pamphlet-waving besuited male – and they mostly are besuited males – as you shop in the supermarket or collect the children at school, try to see beyond the brash exterior. Inside every Ian Paisley is a little boy aiming to please. The rest of us are the same. It's not really our fault, you see. Big boys make us do it. And your votes encourage us.

Vote Yes for Marriage Equality

Two years ago, the 100 members of the Constitutional Convention, meeting in the Grand Hotel in Malahide in north Dublin, delivered a decisive vote of 79 per cent in favour of amending the Irish constitution to provide for marriage equality. The three Sinn Féin delegates voted in favour of amending the constitution to include a positive obligation on the state to give effect to a guarantee of marriage equality and to the equal rights of the children of these marriages. It was described by advocacy groups as 'an historic step' and it was.

But like all such historic steps towards ending discrimination in all its forms and building real equality into society, there has to be a next step and a next step. In January the government finally published the wording for the referendum on same-sex marriage. On 23 May two referenda will be held. One is to reduce the eligibility age for a candidate for the presidential elections. The second is on marriage equality. This referendum vote will decide whether the proposed new wording should be added to the constitution: 'Marriage may be contracted in accordance with law by two persons without distinction as to their sex.'

Early opinion polls indicated that there is an overwhelming majority for a 'Yes' vote. Last December the polls indicated as many as 80 per cent of voters would cast a Yes vote. More recent trends have suggested a small decline in that. An *Irish Times/Ipsos* MRBI poll at the end of March had the Yes side remaining relatively strong at 74 per cent. However, campaigners on both sides are very conscious of the volatility of the electorate and the inaccuracy, on occasion, of polls.

In 2013, opinion polls indicated that the Yes side in the referendum to scrap the Seanad would comfortably win with 62 per cent of the vote. On referendum day, however, the proposal to abolish the Seanad took only 48 per cent of the vote, losing by 4 per cent to the No campaign. So there can be no room for complacency in advance of 22 May. Sinn Féin is for a Yes vote. I would appeal to everyone to vote Yes and I would especially urge Yes voters to become active campaigners for a Yes vote.

Many of us will have a member of our family or extended family who is gay. All of us, whatever age we are or wherever we live or work, know someone who is gay. They are our family, our friends, our workmates and our neighbours. They are of all ages and from all walks of life. They want what we want – the right to live their lives as full and contributing citizens and to share in the love of a family of their own.

There has been a lot of focus on the Easter Rising in recent times. Sinn Féin, the Irish government and many other individuals and organisations have commemorated that historic event and have been setting out their plans for next year's centenary celebrations. At the heart of the Easter Rising is the Proclamation of the Republic. It is the founding document of modern Irish republicanism and for me it is the starting point for my approach to issues of human rights, injustice and inequality. The Proclamation declares that:

> The Republic guarantees religious and civil liberty, equal rights and equal opportunities to all its citizens, and declares its resolve to pursue the happiness and prosperity of the whole nation and of all its parts, cherishing all of the children of the nation equally …

And there you have it. Irish republicans are for equal rights and equal opportunities for all; we are resolved to pursue the happiness of everyone in the nation and to cherish all the children of the nation equally. It does not say unless you are gay or bisexual or transgender. It doesn't say unless you are black or a traveller or a woman or a Catholic or a Protestant. There are no exceptions. It doesn't say whether you are disabled or sick or old. It says *all* its citizens.

The Proclamation wants all of the children of the island of Ireland to be cherished equally and to be happy. Irish republicans want a society which is inclusive and which respects our diversity. Nothing less can be tolerated in a modern, progressive and inclusive society. A lot of progress has been made in recent years. But much more is needed, including tackling the worsening problem of race crime.

On 22 May there is an opportunity to take another historic step forward. I would urge everyone to vote Yes. I would also appeal again for everyone to join the campaign for a Yes vote. If you feel you can't become part of any of the formal campaigns being organised, then become part of the informal campaign. Talk to your friends, to your workmates, to your family and neighbours and ask them to vote Yes. Text them. Facebook them. Use Twitter. Let's get the biggest vote possible and ensure that on 22 May the marriage equality referendum is passed.

Addendum

On 23 May 2015 the result was declared. The people of this state voted by 62 per cent to 38 per cent in favour of marriage equality, and so it became the first state in the world to legalise marriage equality by popular vote.

A Scandal at the Heart
of Government

30 April 2015

Following the economic crash in 2008 two toxic banks in the twenty-six counties – Anglo Irish Bank and Irish Nationwide – were amalgamated into the state-owned Irish Bank Resolution Company (IBRC), which was set up specifically for that purpose. The then Fianna Fáil government handed it the responsibility of managing a range of loans that were in serious trouble, redeeming them if possible or, where necessary, selling them on and getting the best price possible for the taxpayer.

On 18 April 2012 Sinn Féin's finance spokesperson, Pearse Doherty, received a reply from then Minister for Finance Michael Noonan to a question he had asked several weeks earlier about a deal just undertaken by IBRC. This deal concerned loans to a company called Siteserv. Siteserv had borrowed €150 million from Anglo Irish Bank. The company was broke and appeared set to close. The deal, agreed by IBRC, involved the acquisition of Siteserv by Millington, a company owned by businessman Denis O'Brien, for €45.42 million. Seventy per cent of the money Siteserv owed IBRC was written off. The taxpayers lost €105 million on the deal. There was another sting in the tail. Shareholders, including chief executives at Siteserv, received €4.96 million as part of the deal. For a company that was bust!

The taxpayer took a hit of over €100 million, and the shareholders walked away with millions, so Pearse asked the Minister what exactly was going on. Minister Noonan responded with one of those gloriously obnoxious lines that could only be thought up by a Fine Gael, Labour or Fianna Fáil minister: 'Notwithstanding the State's ownership of the bank, IBRC operates at an arm's length capacity from the state in relation to commercial issues.' Basically – 'even though we own the bank, we don't take any interest in what is going on'. That's the line the Irish government has been running with since Freedom of Information requests by Independent TD Catherine Murphy brought a renewed focus onto the Siteserv deal. Political anger and media interest has now put the spotlight on a host of other deals involving IBRC and the writing off of hundreds of millions in taxpayers' money.

In respect of Siteserv we now know that as well as shareholders getting a payment of €5 million to ensure the deal went ahead, the same legal advisers acted for both the purchaser and seller. We also know Michael Noonan was briefed by Department of Finance officials on serious concerns over this transaction and briefed equally on broader concerns over other transactions and the *modus operandi* of IBRC.

Mr Noonan – a former leader of Fine Gael – sat down with Alan Dukes, the chairman of IBRC and also a former leader of Fine Gael to discuss the concerns around the Siteserv sale raised by department officials. Noonan told the Dáil on 23 April 2015 that he had met with Dukes on 25 July 2012, and said:

> The Chairman provided me with strong assurances that the transaction had been thoroughly assessed by the IBRC Board and that the Board of IBRC were satisfied that the transaction was managed in the best manner possible to achieve the best result for the State, including the decision to allow Siteserv to control the sales process.

The Siteserv deal is not the only one that saw debt written down. More than €64 million was written off for Blue Ocean Associates before it was purchased by a consortium. There was an almost 50 per cent write-down of €300 million in debts in the purchase of Topaz.

The Sunday Times ran this story on its front page on Sunday 19 April, but two days later, when challenged on it in the Dáil, Taoiseach Enda Kenny said he had not read the reports. He then appeared to pluck out of the air a suggestion that the comptroller and auditor general could look at the circumstances surrounding the deal to determine whether the taxpayer had received value for money. This was the government trying to kick the issue to touch. Last week in the Dáil I asked the Taoiseach three questions:

1. Why did the Minister for Finance fail to ask the IBRC chairman, Alan Dukes, to conduct a full and independent review of the sale, as recommended by Department of Finance officials?

2. What were the other large transactions conducted by IBRC?

3. Will the government establish an independent commission of investigation of these matters?

The Taoiseach failed to answer these questions.

As it happens it quickly emerged that the comptroller and auditor do not have the authority to investigate Siteserv. The Taoiseach is bound to have known this – so a different approach was needed.

Desperate to avoid a commission of investigation, Minister for Finance Noonan then announced that the special liquidators who helped close IBRC down in 2013 would be asked to review all transactions at IBRC over €10 million. The liquidators are from KPMG, one of the four big world auditors, and we know that when the Siteserv deal was being done the sales process was overseen by KPMG and stockbrokers Davy.

Alan Dukes was not amused and held a press conference at which he said that the Department of Finance was kept abreast of the sales process at all stages.

Last Sunday, new Freedom of Information reports revealed that share activity in Siteserv significantly increased in the month before it was sold off by IBRC and that the share register, which contained the details of those who bought the shares, was given to the liquidator in July 2012. The following day, and in an obvious attempt to defuse public concern about the involvement of KPMG and to avoid having to establish a commission of investigation, the government announced the appointment of a retired High Court judge, Mr Justice Iarfhlaith O'Neill, to oversee 'any actual or perceived conflicts of interests'.

Murkier and murkier. The twists and turns of this story have stayed in the media headlines and there seems to be little prospect of the story going away.

Of course, there is a much wider political issue here centring on Fine Gael, Labour and Fianna Fáil's refusal to ever accept accountability for events that happen on their watch.

But IBRC was not the only government-owned agency handling massive debts arising from the economic crash. The National Asset Management Agency (NAMA) took over much of the debt arising from the collapse of the construction industry and is handling billions in taxpayers' money. Minister Noonan has ordered NAMA to wind up faster than its 2020 remit demands – meaning NAMA is rushing sales processes and there is a lack of transparency there too. Last year, it sold off its entire loan book for the North at an €800 million discount – €800 million the Irish taxpayer will never see again. Irish taxpayers' assets are being disposed of by NAMA at a rate of hundreds of millions of euro every month – and we don't know if we're getting full value for money.

We need an inquiry into what happened in IBRC – during its operation and its liquidation – and that inquiry should include NAMA. The public good and taxpayers' interests require that all transactions, including the acquisition of assets by NAMA, be subjected to thorough independent scrutiny in a commission of investigation.

Addendum

Less than two months after establishing the O'Neill investigation, the government, in June 2015, under pressure, replaced it with a commission of investigation, now chaired by Judge Brian Cregan. As of June 2017 it has yet to publish its final report.

NAMA Scandal

NAMA is once again in the news, this time over the sale of its northern loan portfolio. At the beginning of June, the Irish government was forced into establishing a commission of investigation into the IBRC over concerns about the write-down of debt in the selling off of public assets held by that bank. In the Dáil debate on this I said:

> It's also important to state that the concerns around IBRC are not confined to that bank. Similar concerns surround the operation of the National Asset Management Agency (NAMA).
>
> NAMA also has been handling billions of euro in debts arising from the economic crash, mainly from the collapse of the construction industry. NAMA has been ordered to wind up faster than its 2020 remit demands.
>
> Sinn Féin is concerned that this may result in a failure to get full value for the taxpayer and that NAMA is undertaking a fire sale of assets to meet an arbitrary deadline. So, the distinct impression that citizens are left with after weeks of exposure to the IBRC scandal is that a culture of secrecy exists at the heart of this government.

Mick Wallace TD raised similar and valid concerns around NAMA and the sale of its northern loan portfolio to a US vulture capitalist firm called Cerberus Capital Management back in April 2014. This sale included loans owned by debtors – property developers and investors – from the North who had borrowed from Anglo Irish Bank, AIB and Bank of Ireland. Their loans were secured by assets held across the island of Ireland, Britain and in parts of Europe. The value of these loans had a par value of £4.5 billion and the whole purpose of NAMA selling this loan portfolio – called Project Eagle – was to recoup the losses to the Irish taxpayer who, shamefully, have been forced to bail out the banks that lent the money in the first place. But of course that is not what happened.

What we now know did happen was that NAMA sold the £4.5 billion of loans to Cerberus – it is alleged – for only £1.5 billion. Slowly throughout July accusations emerged that €7 million had been paid to Tughans Solicitors in Belfast by Cerberus. According to Mick Wallace TD, speaking in the Dáil on 2 July 2015, it was 'reportedly earmarked for a Northern Ireland politician or party'. Tughans confirmed that a former partner had moved money without its knowledge, but said it had retrieved it. The UK National Crime Agency launched an investigation and the Assembly agreed to hold an inquiry.

One of the questions of public concern is why did NAMA sell the loans as one lot? Why did it not wait until there was a rise in the northern property market and therefore the value of the assets, in order to get a better return? The whole purpose of NAMA, you will remember, is to recoup the losses to the Irish taxpayer who are burdened with the toxic debt of the bank bail-out at a cost of €64 billion. This in itself is unfair and unjust. Sinn Féin is on the record in the Dáil as having raised our deep concerns about the sale of the 'Project Eagle' loan book from the beginning.

Our finance spokesperson, Pearse Doherty TD, questioned Minister for Finance Noonan on whether or not NAMA had received the best value for the portfolio.

Pearse stated:

Fire sales at the cusp of property price and economic recovery ring every alarm bell there is. [He asked the Minister about] … the number of bidders; the date the bidding process commenced; if he instructed NAMA to dispose of their entire North of Ireland portfolio; the criteria used to establish the successful bidder; and if he will disclose the ultimate price paid for the portfolio.

The Dáil Public Accounts Committee (PAC) then held a hearing on 9 July 2015. The PAC called the NAMA chairman, Frank Daly, and its CEO, Brendan McDonagh, to answer questions about these issues and to probe a series of related events of deepening public concern. Frank Daly told the PAC committee that they first became aware of investor interest in the purchase of the North's loan portfolio when Minister for Finance Noonan gave them a letter he had received from then DUP Minister for Finance Sammy Wilson on 24 June 2013. In that letter Sammy Wilson stated that he had already had discussions with some of those interested in purchasing the loans and that a law firm, Brown Rudnick, had been instrumental in introducing him to these potential investors. Brown Rudnick sent the investors' proposal and he passed it on to Michael Noonan in Dublin for consideration on the same day that he received it, 24 June 2013.

Normally it takes at least ten working days for correspondence to be considered and processed by officials in any department before an advised response is forthcoming from ministers. Anyway, Brown Rudnick stated in that correspondence to Sammy Wilson that, 'Two of our clients have each confirmed that they would, independently, be committed to a process of a potential outright purchase of the NAMA Northern Irish Borrower Connections Loan Book.'

The letter went on to detail a series of conditions expected from their clients. It also stated:

The integrity of the transaction is our main concern. Proceeding, with one party on a limited exclusivity, will ensure a focused, expedient process with guaranteed confidentiality, which we would see as absolutely vital for such a process.

It was a full month later, on 25 July 2013, that Michael Noonan replied to Sammy Wilson. Noonan pointed out that parties interested in acquiring NAMA loans or assets should make direct contact with NAMA themselves. He also said that NAMA's policy was that loan and asset sales should be openly marketed and that it did not favour granting exclusive access to any potential purchaser, as that would militate against achieving optimal value for the assets concerned. A prudent response from Minister Noonan, right?

NAMA informed the PAC that in September 2013 the Brown Rudnick law firm made an unsolicited approach to it to say that their client, PIMCO, was interested in acquiring NAMA's northern loan portfolio, but that they wanted a closed sale, rather than an open one.

This is against NAMA policy. So NAMA engaged with PIMCO, Daly said, to try to persuade them of the merits of an open market approach to the sale.

In early December 2013 PIMCO did make a bid, but still wanted a closed sale. A week later the NAMA board met and decided that the loans would be openly marketed through competitive bidding and a minimum price reserve was agreed which, they claimed, reflected the market value of the assets.

A company called Lazard was appointed by NAMA on 8 January 2014 to oversee the sales process of the loans. However, NAMA then received what was described to the PAC as a 'letter of intent' or memorandum of understanding. This, Daly said, was sent from Peter Robinson through his private office in the

Office of First and Deputy First Minister on 17 January 2014. This letter related to the proposed management of the northern loan portfolio and, according to NAMA, appeared to outline an agreement between PIMCO and the Executive in the North.

This was news to Deputy First Minister Martin McGuinness. It did not have his approval, consent or knowledge.

We now know that on 10 March 2014, PIMCO disclosed to NAMA that they had discovered that their proposed fee arrangement with Brown Rudnick also included the payment of fees to Tughans solicitors and to a former member of NAMA's northern advisory committee, Frank Cushnahan, who had resigned from that committee on 8 November 2013. NAMA have stated that their board met the following day to consider the most appropriate course of action. PIMCO were then told to withdraw from the bidding process by NAMA due to their concerns about the proposed fee arrangement that PIMCO had disclosed to them. We now know from NAMA that this fee was £15m.

Under questioning from Sinn Féin TD Mary Lou McDonald at the PAC, NAMA chairman Frank Daly confirmed that he had alerted Minister Michael Noonan to this serious development on 13 March, including the £15m fee arrangement and how it was to be divided up. Mary Lou then asked the NAMA chairman if the Minister at any stage had a conversation with him about suspending the entire sales process, given this irregularity. Frank Daly confirmed Minister Noonan had not. This is not only astounding, but also ill-judged on the Minister's part. Surely, it was clear that this entire sales process was now flawed and compromised.

It is alarming that Minister Noonan and NAMA did not act to alert the Executive and relevant authorities in the North to this development and their concerns about such an important matter. This failure is unacceptable and requires explanation from Minister Noonan.

Martin McGuinness has written to both Minister Noonan and An Taoiseach Enda Kenny to express his concerns, having only become aware of these matters through the PAC hearing this month. We now know that Lazard had received interest from nine bidders, but it was the US vulture capital fund, Cerberus, who landed the deal. This sale was completed on 20 June 2014.

NAMA stated that, given their concerns around the £15m fee arrangement disclosed by PIMCO, they sought a declaration from Cerberus that nobody connected with NAMA, including any former member of an advisory committee, would be paid any fee, commission or other remuneration or payment in the Project Eagle sales process.

It has since been discovered that Cerberus did contract Brown Rudnick, who in turn used Tughans, and that that firm's managing partner departed the company after a dispute over £7m being diverted to an Isle of Man bank account. That issue is being investigated by the Law Society.

The final commercial deal between NAMA and Cerberus is not yet clear. Ditto whether there were 'fixers' fees paid and if so, to whom exactly? That issue is being investigated by the British National Crime Agency.

For Sinn Féin the core issues are:

- Whether the taxpayer got the best value for money from the sale of Project Eagle.

- Why NAMA and the Minister for Finance, Michael Noonan, failed to abandon the sales process when PIMCO made such a serious disclosure about fixers and fee arrangements.

- Why they then failed to inform the Executive of these serious concerns.

All of this warrants independent examination. This requires the establishment of a commission of investigation by the Irish government. To date the Minister for Finance has failed to even come before the Dáil and make a full statement on the matter. However, Sinn Féin will table a Dáil private members motion at the first opportunity on all these issues. We are therefore putting the government and Minister Noonan on notice.

In the North there also remain outstanding questions, including the concern that there may have been unethical political influence as part of this broader NAMA scandal, as reported widely in the media.

These issues must be fully examined in an open and robust way; otherwise our political institutions risk being brought into disrepute. The Assembly Finance and Personnel Committee have agreed terms of reference and began their first in a series of hearings at Stormont yesterday. The committee have now agreed to invite former DUP Finance Ministers Sammy Wilson and Simon Hamilton to appear before them. They should obviously appear without delay.[1]

The role of Cerberus cannot be ignored either. They must refrain from adding to any negative, downward impact on small businesses, employers and the wider economy, which could occur through a 'fire sale' of assets.

There is rightly a high public expectation that those responsible for inspecting and considering these critical issues – whether law enforcement agencies or Assembly scrutiny committees – will do so in a fair and robust way that ensures the public interest is put first. We can be sure that this is the beginning rather than the end of this saga. There is no doubt that more will come to

---

1   Sammy Wilson gave oral evidence to the Assembly's Finance and Personnel Committee. Simon Hamilton did not.

light from both Dublin and Belfast – and perhaps further – in the time ahead.

Addendum

In May 2017 the government agreed to establish a commission of investigation into NAMA. Following the approval of the draft order by the Dáil and Seanad, the government made the Commission of Investigation (National Asset Management Agency) Order on 13 June 2017. The terms of reference provide for an investigation into Project Eagle.

The Centre Ground
and the Politics of Tweedledee
and Tweedledum

20 October 2016

Following the February 2016 election Fianna Fáil engaged in a long, drawn-out charade of seeking to form a government. It refused to talk to Sinn Féin – as did Fine Gael – and spent weeks posturing. With only forty-four seats in the new Dáil no one believed that Fianna Fáil could secure the necessary support to form a government. But going through the pretence kept them at the centre of lots of media speculation. At one point, under pressure from others in the establishment to end the crisis in government formation, Enda Kenny offered the Fianna Fáil leadership a partnership government. This was a good offer. And a brave one. It was rejected outright. Why?

The fact is there is a genuine nationalist and republican instinct in the grassroots of Fianna Fáil and they want a united Ireland. They know the Fine Gael leadership have no interest in this. Neither does its own leadership at this time but that's another story. An alliance in government between the Blueshirts and the Soldiers of Destiny would leave sections of Fianna Fáil voters looking for a new political home. A republican one, like Sinn Féin. So FF and FG in government was a no go. At least at this time.

But a deal was reached between Fianna Fáil and Fine Gael to form a minority Fine Gael-led government with the help of

Independents. Key to this is a 'confidence and supply' agreement between the two larger parties in which Fianna Fáil agreed to abstain in the election of the taoiseach, the nomination of ministers and the reshuffling of ministers, to facilitate three budgets and to abstain on any motions of no confidence in the government. In return Fine Gael agreed to facilitate Fianna Fáil bills and implement the policy matters set out in the 'confidence and supply' agreement.

Essentially this is a partnership covering all of the key areas of governance including the economy, industrial relations and public sector pay, housing and homelessness, jobs, public services, crime and community services, and putting off a decision on the toxic issue of water charges. This is totally contrary to Fianna Fáil's election manifesto and mandate, as it puts Fine Gael in power with the support and blessing of Fianna Fáil.

The Fianna Fáil leader described this as 'new politics'. It is nothing of the sort. It's all about sustaining the status quo. Liam Mellows, who participated in the 1916 Rising and was summarily executed by the Free State forces during the Civil War, put it well during the Treaty debate in 1922, when he spelled out the consequences of partition. He said: 'Men will get into positions, men will hold power and men who get into positions and hold power will desire to remain undisturbed ...'

However, Budget 2017, which was published in October 2016, also marks another step in the slow, incremental realignment of politics in the south. The common interests of the Fine Gael and Fianna Fáil leaderships crystallised in a clearer way than ever before, so much so that Fianna Fáil never published an alternative budget. Instead they and Fine Gael have been very busy espousing the importance of so-called 'centre ground' politics. In his speech on the budget in the Dáil on 11 October 2016, Minister for Public Expenditure and Reform Paschal Donohoe said:

Those of us in the middle ground of politics have a duty to show that co-operation and consensus can work; to show that our tone can be moderate, but still convincing; and to show that things will not just fall apart and the centre can and will hold, stay firm and will grow.

He was followed minutes later by the Fianna Fáil spokesperson, Michael McGrath, who raised the spectre of the 'extremes'. According to Teachta McGrath:

... the bigger picture is that the centre ground of politics is under attack, not just here in Ireland but throughout Europe, and I agree with the Minister for Public Expenditure and Reform, Deputy Paschal Donohoe, that there are various definitions of centre ground. When one looks at the alternative, one realises just how vital it is that the centre holds.

Later in the Dáil debate, Thomas Byrne of Fianna Fáil returned to the notion of the centrist politics when he claimed that it is the people of Ireland who 'are at the centre of our thinking, as are the policies that will make change happen for them'. Fine Gael Minister Simon Harris took time out of his budget remarks to 'agree with one point made by Deputy Byrne, namely, the one on the centre holding. There are many people on the extreme of Irish politics who would not have thought that we could have delivered a budget and who did not do anything to contribute to that process.'

What does all of this mean? At one level it is about using fear – trying to frighten sections of the electorate into supporting Fine Gael and Fianna Fáil. At another level, it's complete nonsense. Micheál Martin made a play for the centre ground of southern politics in a speech he gave to the MacGill summer school in Glenties, Co. Donegal in July. In it he warned that it is the 'extremes which are setting the terms of the debate' and he spoke of the challenge to 'democratic societies'. Ironically, in his critique of the referendum debate in Britain, and of the Brexiteers, he exposes the very same strategy that Fianna Fáil and Fine Gael are employing to try to see off the challenge from Sinn Féin. Martin accused the British Leave campaign of 'the classic scapegoating of an "other" or a "them" who could be blamed for all discontents'. And he claimed that the campaigners in favour of Brexit exploited the idea that 'if only "we" took back power and "they" were kept out we could discover a glorious past'.

He said this with his brass neck shining brightly in the warm twilight of a Donegal forum. Sounds familiar, doesn't it? This was from the man who has accused Sinn Féin of every conceivable foul deed known to humanity. Operation Fear.

At the same time the Fianna Fáil leader is verbally embracing Sinn Féin's progressive policies. Fairness is the new buzzword. But Budget 2017 is not about fairness and equality. Nor can its politics end the crises in health and housing, or deliver tax fairness, or end water charges. On the contrary Budget 2017 represents the same old doublespeak and political manoeuvring of the past. There is no new politics, just new language for an old story.

The conservative parties remain firmly wedded to an ideology that prefers cuts to capital acquisitions tax for some of the wealthiest citizens in this state rather than investing in the health service. At a time when homelessness is at an historic level and people are being priced out of the rental and first-time buyers' market, Budget 2017 will simply make matters worse. And the budget allocation for a health service in crisis will not resolve the underlying problems.

And none of this takes into account the huge threat to the economy of this island and to society by Brexit.

At a time when the shortcomings of partition are so obvious, the partitionism of the Fianna Fáil and Fine Gael leaderships – the status quo and its maintenance – vindicate Mellow's prophetic warning.

In the Dáil Sinn Féin is the opposition. In policy terms it is Sinn Fein's articulation of radical republican politics and policies that is challenging the conservatism of Fine Gael and Fianna Fáil and Labour. Sinn Féin's politics are embedded in the Proclamation of 1916. We are for economic equality and sustainable prosperity and a new republic that will deliver the highest standard of services and protections for all our citizens. It is these politics and policies that Fine Gael and Fianna Fáil fear.

JUSTICE
FOR ALL

Alice Milligan

20 November 2010

While on hunger strike in 1981 in the prison hospital, Bobby Sands asked if we could get him some of the poems of Alice Milligan. At that time getting a copy of her work was very hard as they had been out of print for many years. However, due to the diligence of our friend Tom Hartley, that great magpie of our struggle, a small hardback book of her poems was found and sent into the H-Blocks. Bobby was delighted. I'm sure Alice Milligan would also have been delighted.

Many moons later Dr Catherine Morris, who is now the Cultural Coordinator for the National Library of Ireland and Trinity College Dublin, wrote an article on Alice Milligan, which I read. It turns out she was researching a book on Milligan. I wrote to her and told her this story. On Wednesday 17 November I was invited by Catherine to go to the National Library for a preview of an exhibition on Milligan entitled 'Alice Milligan and the Irish Cultural Revival'. The exhibition is an impressive, informative and hugely fascinating account of a remarkable woman whose significant contribution to Irish culture, the arts and politics in the late nineteenth and early twentieth century is largely unrecognised. Dr Morris has done a great service to Ireland and to Irish women. She has rewritten Alice Milligan back into our history.

Who was Alice Milligan? She was born in Gortmore outside Omagh in west Tyrone on 4 September 1866. She was the third of thirteen children. A few years later, the family moved to Belfast. It was a unionist household and Alice was educated at Methodist

College and at King's College in London. She trained to be a teacher and for a time taught Latin in Belfast and Derry. She herself said that during this time she 'learned nothing of Ireland'.

In her twenties Alice, along with her father, was part of the Belfast Naturalist Field Club and the Ulster Archaeological Society. It was there that she became a keen photographer and learned how to transfer images onto glass slides for use in public presentations and theatre productions – an early PowerPoint presentation. Her conversion from unionist to radical nationalist occurred when she was twenty-four and living in Dublin. Charles Stewart Parnell's death in 1891 reinforced her conviction in nationalist politics and she threw herself into the emerging Irish language and cultural revival that was then taking place. She was very mindful of the inequalities in Irish society, particularly for women. She derided the fact that in the great debate around the constitutional future of Ireland women were excluded and 'were not called upon to have any opinion whatsoever'.

Alice returned to her family in Belfast. She was determined to pursue her new beliefs, including learning Irish. Undaunted by the anti-Home Rule sentiment around her, Alice and her friends declared their determination to 'lighten the darkness which prevails to such an extent in this province about Irish literature, history and music'. She was described as the 'red-headed nationalist' and a 'black mark' on her family's name.

In 1895 Milligan and Anna Johnson founded *The Northern Patriot* and then the *Shan Van Vocht* – taken from the Irish *An tSean Bhean Bhocht* – the poor old woman – a representation of Ireland. Both were hugely influential publications. The two women wrote much of the content, including poems, songs and political essays, and encouraged new writers and thinkers. James Connolly received his first commission to write in an Irish publication from the *Shan Van Vocht*.

Alice Milligan was also a prime mover in the centenary celebrations in Belfast to mark the hundredth anniversary of the 1798 Rising. She was part of the 'Ardrigh group', a loose affiliation of republicans and nationalists who came together at the writer and historian Francis Joseph Bigger's home, 'Ardrigh' on the Antrim Road, to discuss politics and agree ways to promote the Irish language and culture. Milligan was at the centre of all of this, including writing the biography *Life of Theobald Wolfe Tone*. She was also involved in the establishment of a wide range of other groups, among them the Henry Joy McCracken Literary Society, the Women's Centenary Union and branches of the Irish Women's Association. She was a prolific writer in local journals and newspapers.

Milligan and her friends understood the threat that existed to the Irish language and culture. British policy was to destroy both in order to destroy the Irish identity and sense of national pride. In retaliation Milligan and her friends encouraged festivals and language classes, and promoted drama and the Gaelic League. Her pioneering work in the theatre helped forge the connection between drama, the theatre and the Irish language. She wrote dramas, produced plays and toured widely throughout the country with these dramas.

Thomas MacDonagh, who was one of the signatories of the Proclamation and was executed in 1916, recognised the immense contribution of Alice Milligan. In the *Irish Review* of September 1914 he wrote:

> I will begin with the best … It is meet [appropriate] that this Irish National poet should be a woman. It is meet that she, like so many of the Irish Volunteers, should be of North East Ulster. Alice Milligan, Ulster Protestant, Gaelic Leaguer, Fenian, friend of all Ireland, lover of Gaelic Catholics as of her own kith … Alice Milligan is the most Irish of living poets and therefore the best.

She was a friend of most of the leaders of republican and nationalist politics and the Irish language movement. She campaigned tirelessly on behalf of Roger Casement and attended his trial in London every day. After his execution she spent time visiting Irish political prisoners being held in English jails. She also increasingly took on the role of carer for members of her family. She moved back to the North and settled outside of Omagh and continued to write and campaign. In the late 1920s she helped establish the Anti-Partition Union. She died in 1953.

Alice Milligan was a passionate, gifted and articulate advocate for Ireland. She loved Ireland and the Irish people and her contribution to all aspects of Irish society was immense. It is fitting that each Easter members of the Milligan–Harte Sinn Féin Cumann in west Tyrone lay a wreath at her graveside in memory of this great Irish woman.

Write on Ma!

6 August 2009

During the 2009 Féile I wandered into St Mary's University College on the Falls Road and through the main exhibitions. All of them were brilliant. That aspect of the Féile goes back to almost the first Féile an Phobail held in 1988. Paintings, artwork, photographic exhibitions, sculptures, quilts – every Féile has had unique and very striking examples of the visual arts.

The artist Robert Ballagh, a long-standing friend of the Féile, exhibited his remarkable work here. So did Jim Fitzpatrick and many, many others. Some of the exhibitions are of times past. A good example of that for the 2009 Féile was the exhibition about Belfast dockers. And there was Gerry Collins' Bombay Street photos.

There was also an exhibition by the families of the eleven people killed in Ballymurphy between 9–11 August 1971 when the British government introduced internment. These families are looking for:

- An independent international investigation examining the circumstances surrounding all of the deaths.

- The British government to issue a statement of innocence and a public apology.[1]

---

1   Incidentally, in May 2017, forty-six years later, the Belfast High Court finally set a date, 11 September 2018, for the inquest into the Ballymurphy killings. If you are interested in contacting 'The Ballymurphy Massacre Committee' you can do so through their website: www.ballymurphymassacre.com.

Their exhibition drew me in and I began looking at the photographs of the victims and other artefacts from that time. A handwritten statement grabbed my attention. The writing looked vaguely familiar. It was my mother's! It was a complaint against the British Army, written a few days after internment was introduced. We lived at 11 Divismore Park at that time. The British Army had targeted the house constantly. Indeed, they used to run their heavily armoured Saladin and Saracen cars against the walls of the house. A combination of that and the bad design and structure meant that the house was demolished and there is now a shop where we used to live.

I remember when I was a child, perhaps seven or eight, accompanying her as she lobbied local political representatives for a house. Since she and my father had married, they and our growing family had lived with other family members or in a private rented tenement. A number of other families shared this slum with us. Eventually she succeeded in being allocated a house in Ballymurphy and she and my granny went there one day to view the site. I was with them and I recall as we walked across the building site one of the workmen showing her where her new home would be.

On 9 August 1971 I watched the paratroopers raid our home. I was nearby in Springhill Avenue. My father and one of my younger brothers were among the several hundred men from across the North arrested that morning. I hadn't slept at home since 1969, except for the odd night.

All of this came back to me as I read her statement. My mother's matter-of-fact account of the behaviour of the British Army says it better than anything I could write about what she and other women put up with during the raids. The damage to the house was so bad during that internment raid that my mother moved out – never to return. She's dead now but she often used to say that 11 Divismore Park was the place in which she had been happiest.

This is her 'Complaints against the [British] Army' form:

Name and address of complainant: Mrs Annie Adams,
    11, Divismore Pk. (Present Address: 8, Kerrykeel Gdns)

Occupation: Housewife

Date of alleged offence: 10th August 1971   Time: 3–4 a.m.

Place of alleged offence: 11, Divismore Park

Details of alleged offence: Damage to property, theft.

Damages to house: Slashed head board of divan – 'Britain for ever' written on it. Slashed 2 mattresses, destroyed clock, T.V. and radiogram. Smashed pictures on the wall and removed 2 pictures (Barnes & McCormack & 1916 Proclamation.) Robbed gas meter. Stole bracelet (£8) and transistor radio. A clock also taken. Destroyed food stuffs and clothing. Pulled cupboards off the sink units. Took the alsatian with them (supposed to be at Paisley Pk on West Circular). The military took over the house and gave me 10 minutes to get out of it. As we were leaving soldiers in a Saracen fired shots in the air to frighten us and laughed. I am now squatting in 8 Kerrykeel Gardens. The military have now left my home at Divismore Park. The ceilings of the 2 bedrooms were broken through by soldiers in the roof space.

They have continually prosecuted me since 1969. My husband is interned and my two sons are on the run.

Complaint made to Henry Taggart Hall. They denied any responsibility and said, 'It must have been your Irish B's.'

Identification of Military: Paratroopers.

Complaint made to military: Yes. Protest by 200 women who saw damage.

Name, rank and unit of soldier to whom complaint made: Could be identified – complaint made at Henry Taggart [Hall] & also Springfield RIC Bks.

Solicitor notified: Yes. Mr McCann of Garvey, Lynch and McClean [?], Castle Lane

Witnesses: All neighbours.

Signature: Annie Adams   Date: 26th August 1971
[Witnessed] E. Watson

Symphysiotomy –
Righting a Grievous Wrong

15 March 2012

The public gallery was abnormally packed for a Thursday morning in the Dáil. It's not unusual to have groups of young people from schools visiting to watch proceedings, but almost all of those present this morning were elderly women. Another large group of women were in an adjacent room where they were watching proceedings on TV. These women are the survivors of a barbaric medical practice called symphysiotomy. For the first time, on 15 March 2012, the Dáil was listening to statements on the use of symphysiotomy.

Symphysiotomy amounts to institutional abuse, involving acts of butchery against women citizens. It is a painful, dangerous operation that unhinges the pelvis to facilitate childbirth or, in the case of pubiotomy, the sawing of the pubic bones. Some have sought to claim that it was a standard practice internationally but the facts contradict this. The French medical profession abandoned its use in 1798, over 200 years ago. It was regarded as too dangerous to mother and child, many of whom died. The French opted for Caesarean section. It took the British another seventy years to catch on to its dangers. But in the Irish state symphysiotomy was the method of choice between the 1940s and early 1980s. During that time, it is thought that up to 1,500 women were victims of this procedure, mostly without their consent. It was also inflicted on women who were used as teaching aids for doctors, nurses and students. One hospital that used it extensively was Our Lady of Lourdes Hospital in Drogheda, run by the Medical Missionaries of Mary, who exported the use of this practice to Africa and India through those religious nurses it trained.

I had never heard of symphysiotomy and pubiotomy until just over a year ago when I made the shift to Louth. It was brought to my attention by two very brave women, Olivia Kearney and Catherine Naughton, who are both women of great grace and courage. Since then I have met other victims and survivors, including the advocacy groups. They are all remarkable people. Last night a group of survivors – Matilda Behan, Ellen Moore and Helen Kennealy – and Anne Ward, who spoke on behalf of her mother, Mary MacDonogh, gave witness and harrowing testimony to the hurt and trauma of symphysiotomy. Their accounts were deeply distressing and upsetting for those who gave them and for us who listened in silence.

Those who have campaigned on this issue for many years at-tribute its use by the medical profession in the South to Catho-lic Church dogma. The Catholic hierarchy vehemently opposed birth control methods and the use of Caesarean sections limited the number of children a woman could have. It was generally accepted that the maximum number of these that could be done was four. The use of symphysiotomy was one way of ensuring that women didn't look to birth control.

Today there are probably no more than 200 or so survivors of symphysiotomy. They are elderly and frail citizens who carry the physical and emotional scars of this barbaric practice. Those courageous women have all suffered long-term ill health and disability as a consequence of what was done to them.

One woman who called to see me in Drogheda to tell me of her experience was Lilly McDonnell. Lilly was a victim of sym-physiotomy sixty years ago. She told me how her child was killed in the course of this procedure and of the physical damage done to her. She showed me the child's birth certificate. Like the other survivors, Lilly has never forgotten what happened to her and her child.

The state should be deeply ashamed of what it allowed to happen to these women because of, in my view, the influence of conservative religious fundamentalism. It should also be ashamed of its inadequate and, at times, heartless response to the demands of the victims for redress and truth. In their efforts to highlight what was done to them the victims frequently met a wall of misinformation and institutionalised obstruction. Records were destroyed or 'lost' and the aftercare that they deserved was denied if they could not prove, by the presentation of medical records, what had been done to them.

The Dáil and Seanad and the government has a duty to ensure that this deep wrong is finally brought to a conclusion and in a way that is acceptable to the victims. In a real republic the rights of these citizens would have been protected and the survivors of symphysiotomy would have had justice many years ago.

Deputy James Reilly gave his full support to the demand for a public inquiry at an Oireachtas committee hearing in 2009. Now he is Minister for Health, with the responsibility and the power to finally make it happen. He can authorise a full public inquiry into these events. Nothing else will suffice. Nothing else will do. Without this the campaigning, but more importantly the hurt, the anguish, the grief and the bereavement for the victims, will go on.

Looking up at the public gallery this morning the faces looking down were of women grievously treated and ignored for decades and who are now mostly in their late seventies and early eighties. As each Teachta Dála stood and spoke, they listened intently. Following the Minister's opening remarks, Caoimhghín

Ó Caoláin, who is the leader of the all-party group – made up of representatives of all of the parties in the Dáil – on this issue, and who has championed this campaign for many years, was the next to speak.

There was spontaneous applause from the public gallery when he finished. And the speaker after that was applauded. Those who have been marginalised and whose pain was ignored were responding warmly to their issue finally being debated in the Dáil. And when it was all over Caoimhghín sought the indulgence of the Leas-Ceann Comhairle and asked those TDs present to stand and applaud the women. It was a rare emotional moment of unanimity in a chamber normally given over to the cut and thrust of verbal political battle.

But it can't end here. The Dáil and the government has to deliver for the victims and their families. The state has thus far refused to apologise to these women, presumably to avoid being held legally accountable. I believe that with political will the government can be made to deliver for the victims. I am also convinced that a number of other justice campaigns can be resolved in this term of the Dáil. They include justice for the 'Maggies' (victims of the Magdalene Laundries) and for other victims of institutionalised abuse, including in Bethany Home and our Lady of Lourdes Hospital, Drogheda. All these causes are crying out for justice. We can do something about it. These women as citizens deserve our support and our love, and they particularly deserve to have their wrongs righted.

Addendum

Following the publication of the Walsh Report in 2014, the Murphy Report in 2014 and the publication in November 2016 of the report by Judge Maureen Harding Clark on the Surgical Symphysiotomy Ex-gratia Payment Scheme, most of the victims agreed to compensation. Some are continuing with court cases seeking compensation. The state has yet to make an apology to the victims.

Slavery and the Magdalene Laundries

8 October 2012

Did you know that there are an estimated twenty-seven million slaves in the world today? I didn't. Many are forced labourers and soldiers – many of them children – coerced, sold and traded into involuntary service, and over half of forced labourers and almost all of sex trafficking victims are women and young girls.

In the language of the twenty-first century the word slavery has been largely replaced with the term 'human trafficking' or 'trafficking in persons'. But it is still slavery. It takes many forms, from sexual exploitation to the use of forced labour in sweatshops and working long hours in factories. And modern slavery is not confined to the developing world, as trafficking in persons is a serious problem in the developed world. For example, according to recent statistics from the US State department at least 14,500 people are trafficked into the USA every year.

For many the notion of slavery is linked to the slave ships that plied their trade across the Atlantic between Africa and the USA, or the American Civil War (1861–65) that freed the slaves but didn't bring freedom or equality or justice for many generations. There were Irish slaves, too. Thousands were sold by the British in the seventeenth century to the plantations in the Caribbean, while many more were indentured servants – little better than slaves. But the realisation that slavery today is a world-wide phenomenon that continues to exist in many countries is a surprise.

Each year I attend the Clinton Global Initiative (CGI) conference in New York run by former President Bill Clinton. The CGI brings together non-governmental organisations, business and political leaders and governments. It seeks to raise money and build partnerships that can address specific issues of concern in education, healthcare and employment training. Most of its activities are focused on developing nations. Each year the issue of human trafficking and in particular of women and young girls, and the conditions of their employment and exploitation as sex workers, is the subject of debate. I was there in September 2012 and this issue was given added weight on the final day of the CGI in a speech by President Obama, who dedicated his entire remarks to the issue of modern slavery:

> When a man, desperate for work, finds himself in a factory or on a fishing boat or in a field, working, toiling, for little or no pay, and beaten if he tries to escape – that is slavery. When a woman is locked in a sweatshop, or trapped in a home as a domestic servant, alone and abused and incapable of leaving – that's slavery. When a little boy is kidnapped, turned into a child soldier, forced to kill or be killed – that's slavery. When a little girl is sold by her impoverished family – girls my daughters' age – runs away from home, or is lured by the false promises of a better life, and then imprisoned in a brothel and tortured if she resists – that's slavery. It is barbaric, and it is evil, and it has no place in a civilized world.

On the same day that Obama made his remarks, Sinn Féin introduced a Private Members Motion into the Dáil to help the victims of a form of slavery that for many decades passed unnoticed in the Irish state and which even today this Irish government is failing to deal with properly.

The Magdalene asylums first opened their doors in Ireland

approximately 200 years ago. The first was opened by the Church of Ireland in Dublin, initially seeking to 'rehabilitate' prostitutes. Those run by Catholic religious orders lasted the longest. Over time, the state increasingly used these institutions as a place to deal with a multitude of social problems, including poverty, disability, so-called immoral behaviour, babies born out of wedlock, domestic and sexual abuse, youth crime and infanticide. The religious orders in turn used these girls and women as unpaid labour. The last operating laundry closed its doors on Sean MacDermott Street in Dublin in 1996, with forty women still in residence, the eldest of them seventy-nine, the youngest in her forties.

Women incarcerated in these institutions worked for no pay whilst the orders ran the laundries on a commercial basis in brutally harsh conditions. There were ten laundries in Dublin, Waterford, Limerick, Cork, Galway and Wexford, and the state provided direct and indirect financial support.

The Ryan Report (2009) details the women's forced unpaid labour and states that their working conditions were harsh, they were completely deprived of their liberty and suffered both physical and emotional abuse. Those who tried to escape and were caught by the garda were returned to the institutions.

The Magdalene women were excluded by the state from the 2002 Residential Institutions Redress Scheme established to pay victims of abuse in church-run institutions like the industrial school system, primarily on the basis that the laundries were privately run. The state claimed it had no involvement in the institutions.

In June 2011 the government set up an interdepartmental committee into the Magdalene Laundries for the purpose of clarifying any state interaction with the laundries. Senator Martin McAleese was appointed chair of the committee. A Sinn Féin Dáil motion in September 2012 was intended to support the work of the McAleese committee and to persuade the government to take steps to alleviate some of the trauma still being suffered by these women, all of whom are elderly. The motion was supported by seventeen independent TDs and highlighted the huge injustice done to the women of the Magdalene Laundries, and the hurt and hardship caused by their exclusion from the Residential Institutional Redress Scheme. The motion called for immediate and meaningful discussion on an apology and a redress scheme, and for the government to provide the funding for and implementation of a helpline for the survivors of the Magdalene Laundries. The government defeated the motion.

In opposition both Labour and Fine Gael criticised the Fianna Fáil government for excluding both the Magdalene Laundries and Bethany Home from the redress scheme. Yet when they were in government subsequently, they questioned the established facts surrounding the treatment of the women.

But the facts are well known and have been graphically presented in previous reports, including some by international agencies, by the survivors and in a recent report produced by the Justice for the Magdalenes organisation. These women endured slavery and successive Irish governments colluded in this. That was shameful. But it is even more dishonourable that this government should fail to resolve this issue and chose instead to add hurt to the victims by doubting their veracity.

I recently read a poem, 'Still I Rise', by Maya Angelou. It relates to the slavery of African-Americans but isn't exclusive to them. It says so much about the courage and heroism of those of whatever colour who resist slavery and determine to rise above it. As I read it, I thought of the women and girls of the Magdalene Laundries.

You may write me down in history
With your bitter, twisted lies,

You may trod me in the very dirt
But still, like dust, I'll rise.

Addendum

In 2013 Taoiseach Enda Kenny apologised to the women who had been held in the Magdalene Laundries. However, significant controversy still surrounds the laundries, including details on the exact number of women who died in them. In June 2017 the Dublin High Court ruled that two former industrial school residents who were excluded from the Magdalene compensation scheme had been denied fair procedures by the Department of Justice. This opens up the cases of others denied compensation. The Ombudsman has also launched a full investigation into whether the redress scheme has been administered properly by the Department of Justice.

Violence against Women: a Cause and Consequence of Women's Inequality

4 July 2013

The recent conviction of Adrian Bayley in Australia for the brutal rape and murder of Irish native Jill Meagher, as well as the savage murder of Jolanta Lubiene and her eight-year-old daughter Enrika in Co. Kerry, have all brought into focus the issue of violence against women. Coincidentally, in June the annual report for 2012 from Women's Aid was published. Its facts were equally shocking:

- One in five women in the Irish state will experience violence and abuse from an intimate partner.

- 3,230 disclosures of direct child abuse were made to the Women's Aid helpline – a 55 per cent increase on the previous year.

- 11,729 calls were made to the freephone helpline. That's 32 calls per day.

- 49 per cent of the women supported in One to One service were experiencing abuse from a former husband, partner or boyfriend. [One to One provides in-depth information support on a one-to-one basis with women experiencing domestic violence.]

- 30 per cent of first-time One to One support visits were with women from migrant communities.

- The most dangerous time can be when a woman is planning or making her exit and in the period afterwards.

The facts are equally stark in the North. The 'Making the Grade' report in 2007 revealed that:

- In 2006–07 the PSNI responded to a domestic incident every twenty-two minutes of every day.

- In 2006–07 there were more domestic violence-related crimes (10,115) than the combined total for sexual offences against children, indecent exposure, robbery, armed robbery, hijacking, fraud and counterfeiting, shoplifting, dangerous driving offences and firearms offences.

- 20 per cent of all attempted murders in 2006–07 had a domestic motivation.

- The rate of conviction for rape decreased from 28.2 per cent in 1994 to 19 per cent in 2005.

- The number of recorded rapes increased from 292 in 2001 to 457 in 2006.

- 84 per cent of victims of sexual offences were women.

But as with all statistics it is essential that you look beyond the bullet points and focus on the human experiences that they reflect.

The Women's Aid report records harrowing accounts. Women have described being locked in and prevented from leaving their houses, being drugged, assaulted and hospitalised, being beaten while pregnant or breast-feeding, being gagged to stop them screaming, being raped and sexually abused, including being pinned down and assaulted, and being forced to have sex in return for money to feed their children.

For women, violence includes, but is not limited to, domestic violence, forced marriage, rape and sexual assault, crimes in the name of honour, murder, trafficking and sexual exploitation, female genital mutilation, sexual harassment and stalking. It causes physical damage ranging from death to miscarriages to broken limbs. Sexual offences can also result in sexually transmitted diseases and forced pregnancies, as well as leaving long-term psychological damage.

Kofi Annan, the former head of the United Nations said:

> Violence against women is perhaps the most shameful human rights violation and it is perhaps the most pervasive. It knows no boundaries of geography, culture or wealth. As long as it continues we cannot claim to be making real progress towards equality, development and peace.

Safe Ireland, which works with frontline domestic violence services across the state to provide state-of-the-art and sustainable responses to women and children experiencing domestic violence, also published the results of a one-day survey across the Irish state on 6 November 2012, which revealed that almost 850 women and children received support and protection from domestic violence over a single twenty-four-hour period. The survey found that more than 500 women and over 300 children sought domestic violence services on that day. Almost 270 women and children were accommodated in refuges, with twenty-one women being turned away due to lack of space. The census also found that more than twenty pregnant women looked for safety from violence.

At its core, violence against women is a cause and a consequence of women's inequality. It cannot be challenged and defeated without an acknowledgement of this. So how do we end it? Coherent, integrated and properly economical social, cultural and political strategies are needed. Such strategies do work.

Addendum

Regrettably the promised consolidated domestic violence legislation contained in the Programme for Government 2011 has yet to be delivered. Six years later, in May 2017, I again asked about this in the Dáil. I was told that the Bill has reached committee stage in the Seanad.

The bottom line is that there is no underlying strategic approach or priority being given to this issue. So, we can have rushed legislation on property rights to aid banks but no legislation on property rights to help women victims of violence. And all the while violence against women continues.

In the years since this column was written the situation for women has worsened. In its Impact Report summary for 2016 for the twenty-six counties, which was published in May 2017, Women's Aid reported:

- 3,823 disclosures of child abuse.

- 19,115 contacts with Women's Aid direct services.

- 20,769 disclosures of domestic violence against women and children.

The annual report of 2015–16 for the Women's Aid Federation in the North reported:

- 738 women and 520 children stayed in refuge – 267 women couldn't access it because it was full.

- 6,212 women and 7,296 children accessed outreach support.

- 25,935 calls to twenty-four-hour domestic and sexual violence helpline.

- Domestic violence accounted for 13.4 per cent of all crime reported to the PSNI.

- Police responded to a domestic incident every nineteen minutes.

The Shame of Direct Provision

10 October 2014

There was a time when the holiday camp at Mosney hosted the likes of Joe Dolan and Dickie Rock. Thousands danced the night away to 'You're Such a Good-Looking Woman' and 'The House with the Whitewashed Gable'. Sadly Joe is no longer with us, but Dickie is still going strong. So too is Mosney. I was there only once. Years ago. Maggie McArdle, God rest her, my favourite mother-in-law, was on a Senior Citizens Weekend Away and we called to visit her. The place was buzzing. Maggie really enjoyed her holiday. So did many others over the decades. When he heard I was to visit Mosney once again, Dessie Ellis TD regaled me with tales of his amorous adventures and countless more innocent Dublin family breaks at Mosney.

These days Mosney is an Asylum Accommodation Centre. Seanadóir Trevor Ó Clochartaigh, Councillor Eimear Ferguson and I visited it on Friday last. A letter to Trevor from the Reception and Integration Agency (RIA), which is responsible for the overall provision of accommodation and support for refugees and asylum seekers, set out the conditions for our visit. They included a prohibition on media accompanying the delegation, any advance announcement of the visit and a prohibition on 'live tweeting' during the visit. I don't know the legal basis for these conditions but, with what is probably a former prisoner's instinct, I tweeted anyway. Just out of contrariness. Interestingly I notice that a visit by President Michael D. Higgins to an accommodation centre for asylum seekers was cancelled recently after the Department of Justice allegedly refused permission for the event on the grounds of 'logistics and safety'.

The camp at Mosney is massive. It is well maintained and clean. There are lots of trees and green spaces. The management team who accompanied us were hospitable, friendly and courteous. Some of the residents said Mosney is one of the better centres, not least because they have privacy. Some hostels are cramped and have communal toilets. There are 602 people in Mosney. Those we met are focused on getting out of there, some of whom are waiting ten years. It is an indictment of the government and its predecessor that this is the case. Direct Provision is an inhumane system. No matter how 'attractive' the accommodation may be, the system institutionalises people, damages their mental health and forces idleness on them.

Direct Provision is a system that is meant to provide for the welfare needs of asylum seekers and their families. It does not. It provides a measly €15.60 a week for each child. What child can be cared for on €15.60 a week? At the end of September 2014 there were 4,336 in the Direct Provision system. 614 have been there for more than five years. There were also 1,666 children living in this system. Many of the children were born here. Many are denied citizenship. Most have spent their entire childhoods in the system.

Minister of State for Equality Aodhán Ó Ríordáin says a new inspection regime for conditions in Direct Provision Centres is urgently needed. Fair enough. All our systems need to be properly run with legislative regulations in place. But the Direct Provision system needs to be abolished, as it has no legislative basis whatsoever. It was a rush job by Fianna Fáil back in 1999, compiled without proper accountability and poor institutional oversight. Since 2000, private contractors who run the centres have been paid €900 million of taxpayers' money.

There is no need to wait for Immigration, Residence and

Protection legislation to be passed in order to put a stop to Direct Provision. Other states deal with immigrants in a much more humane, efficient and less costly way. There is no reason why this cannot happen here. The people in Direct Provision have rights. Our delegation met a group – mostly of women – during our visit. All of them want to contribute to Irish society; instead they are denied the right to work. They are segregated, unable to participate in any meaningful way. We also met local people who work on a voluntary basis to assist these 'new Irish', especially the children.

There is no excuse for the wasted creative human potential that is currently unused in Direct Provision centres. There is no excuse for treating human beings like this. Some of us campaign on behalf of Irish emigrants in the USA and other countries. If our citizens were being treated the way we treat our immigrants, Irish politicians would – rightly! – be raising a row about it. All thinking people were horrified at the horrors inflicted on children and women in Industrial Schools, Mother and Baby Homes and Magdalene Laundries. Politicians from all parties and none expressed outrage. These scandals happened because that's the way the system worked. So too today with Direct Provision.

All of the residents we met at Mosney were dark-skinned. Most were from Africa. Could this be why our system treats them in a way that denies their humanity, their rights and the great contribution they and their children could make to our island community?

Addendum

At the end of April 2017 there were 4,617 people residing in the thirty-four state-provided accommodation centres. Of these, 1,233 were children and 27 were over the age of sixty-six. There were 467 children up to the age of four, 585 between five and twelve, and 181 between thirteen and seventeen.

A total of 1,773 people, or 38.4 per cent, were in Direct Provision for under twelve months. 1,291 people were there between one and two years. 645 were in accommodation for between two and three years, 327 people for between three and four years, 183 for between four and five years, 157 for between five and six years, 83 for between six and seven years, and 318 for seven years plus.

A Sea Change in Attitude towards Travellers is Needed

25 October 2015

Funerals can occasionally be surprisingly joyous events, a celebration of the life of someone who has lived it to the full and made a unique contribution to family, community or society. But mostly they are sad. Last week was a particularly sad time for funerals as there were two distressing funerals for the ten victims of the Carrickmines fire at a temporary Travellers halting site. On Tuesday 20 October 2015 I was in Bray for the funerals of Tara Gilbert, her partner Willy Lynch, their daughters Jodie (9) and Kelsey (4), and Willy's brother Jimmy. Two days later I was in Sandyford for the funerals of Sylvia and Thomas Connors and their children Jimmy (5), Christy (2) and Mary (5 months). Sylvia was the sister of Willy and Jimmy Lynch. Ten members of one family were gone in a few brief minutes of horror – five adults and five children. The haunting, beautiful laments of a lone uilleann piper echoed over the church grounds and the nearby car park of a shopping centre as Mary Lou McDonald and I arrived.

Sylvia, Willy and Jimmy's brother John spoke at Thursday's funeral. His voice frequently broke as he tried to hold back the raw emotion evident on his face. He described the last day they had all been together. 'We had a lovely day. The kids were playing in my garden … But the next morning came the call. I thought it was a hoax call. Then, in a moment, I realised all my family was gone. My brothers, my sister, my sister-in-law, my brother-in-law, my nephews and nieces. The whole lot gone in one go.'

Mary Lou and I and local Sinn Féin councillors and activists were there to extend our condolences and solidarity to the Lynch, Gilbert and Connors families and to the Traveller community. But it is time that Irish society went beyond mere sympathy and solidarity. The treatment of the Traveller community by the settled community over many centuries has been poor. The response of governments and the health and educational institutions of the state has been equally poor.

In the North, nationalists were treated as second-class citizens for longer than the existence of the northern state. The Orange state was a place in which sectarianism and discrimination in housing and jobs and political representation was endemic. It was an apartheid state. Almost two decades after the Good Friday Agreement, we are still trying to reverse the social, economic and political legacy of the policies and attitudes that led to that. That is why equality and parity of esteem are so fundamental to the process.

But Travellers have been treated as even less than that and the prejudice and discrimination they face has, if anything, worsened over the years. The opposition to the erection of a temporary halting site for those bereaved by the Carrickmines fire is deeply disappointing. The decision to provide the families with a site on a parking lot that is inadequate for their needs and which lacks basic amenities is an indictment of this and successive governments and their inaction in providing for the needs of the Traveller community.

Some people in the settled community blame Travellers for anti-social behaviour, crime and other misconduct. But even if some Travellers – like some in the settled community – behave badly, that is no reason to demonise and exclude an entire community.

What must be acknowledged is that ignorance breeds fear. The only cure for that is education and engagement. It's about people getting to know each other and learning to respect and tolerate one another. Travellers are citizens. They have rights. Those rights are being denied to them. Travellers are among the most socially marginalised and disadvantaged groups in Irish society today.

These citizens fare badly in all key indicators of disadvantage, including employment, poverty, health, infant mortality, life expectancy, literacy, education and accommodation. Many Travellers are forced to endure intolerable, substandard living conditions, with around a third living without access to basic facilities such as sanitation, water and electricity, leading to widespread health problems among Travellers. Unemployment within the community is huge. Most estimates put it around 75 per cent. A Traveller's life expectancy is significantly reduced by as much as fifteen years compared to those in the settled community. Cutbacks in education, health and other services have also impacted severely on the Traveller community. The suicide rate is six times that of the settled community.

At the root of all these problems are the unacceptable levels of prejudice, discrimination and social exclusion experienced by Travellers at institutional and other levels. Fundamentally, Travellers are not treated as full and equal citizens. There is an underlying racism at work that has created a form of apartheid. This is at odds with the generosity and inclusiveness expressed by Irish society in the recent marriage equality campaign, or the solidarity demonstrated with refugees from the Middle East, or the amazing amounts of money raised each year by charities for international relief programmes.

The widespread expressions of sympathy following the fire that killed ten people, including five children, at the temporary halting site on Glenamuck Road provided hope that this situation could begin to turn around. Unfortunately that hope has been dented by the reappearance of familiar negative attitudes and problems as attempts have been made to re-house the families of the victims of this tragedy. What this has underlined is the need for an urgent, far-reaching and fundamental reappraisal of the way in which Travellers are treated in Irish society.

In April 2014 the Oireachtas Joint Committee on Justice, Defence and Equality recommended that this state recognises the ethnicity of the Traveller community. The government needs to build on the solidarity which has been evident since the Carrickmines fire, by demonstrating political leadership and declaring that the state recognises Traveller ethnicity. Of course, such a development would not of itself solve the problems which confront the Traveller community but it would demonstrate leadership on this issue by the government and set a clear and positive example.

But much more needs to be done. I believe that we now need to establish a national forum, across the island of Ireland, involving Travellers and the settled community, including representatives of all political parties, of government, local authorities, health and education sectors and representatives of media organisations, so that we may plan a way forward. Such a forum would discuss openly and in detail how discrimination and prejudice against Travellers can be confronted, including prejudicial attitudes facilitated by the actions of some politicians and media outlets. It would examine and make recommendations on how the wider community can be educated about Traveller culture.

Last week, when I put this to the Taoiseach in the Dáil he rejected it. His view is that the existing structures can meet this need. Patently, judging from the statistics available, they cannot. If we are to build an inclusive society in which equality is real and meaningful, and not something that is occasionally given lip service, then we need a sea change in attitudes and legislation.

Travellers must be treated and regarded as full and equal citizens of Ireland. This will only happen with political leadership and must be led by government.

Addendum

On 1 March 2017 the government announced that it was formally recognising the Traveller community as an ethnic group. This decision, belated though it was, is a step in the right direction. It was a very historic moment for the 40,000 members of the Traveller community and is an important symbolic acknowledgement, but it must also pave the way for real, practical change. We need to keep moving in that direction. Action must follow.

An All-Ireland Suicide
Strategy is Essential

8 September 2016

There is not a single family across this island that has not been affected by the challenge of mental health issues. It is now accepted that one in seven adults will experience mental health issues in any given year. Allied to this is the issue of suicide. It is now believed that the real figures for suicide across the island of Ireland are as high as 1,000 people annually. The under-reporting of suicide has always been a problem. Often deaths resulting from road accidents and drowning are impossible to classify.

The reality is that all sections and all generations of our society are affected, from the very young to the very old, and in rural and urban areas. Self-harming is also a huge issue. Thousands are admitted to hospitals every year due to self-harming, which in many cases goes unreported.

The impact on families and communities is huge. Most are left wondering: why? They are left asking what they could have done to prevent the death of a loved one. The emotional trauma is enormous. In the aftermath of a suicide, especially of a young person, the danger of others also taking their own lives is high. I still remember visiting the wake homes of four young victims from the Upper Springfield area in west Belfast in October 2010 who had all died from suicide within days of each other.

There is no single or easy explanation for someone deciding to take their life. In my experience the reasons can be many – mental health problems, loneliness, bullying, alcohol and substance misuse, an absence of hope for the future. There is, however, a clear and direct correlation between deprivation and suicide. Every statistical analysis that I have read shows areas of high unemployment and deprivation suffer greater levels of suicide. At the same time, suicide is no respecter of class or age or gender.

The investigative online news website *The Detail* reported that there were 318 suicides registered in the North in 2015. This was, it said, the highest annual death rate in forty-five years and it means that, on average, six people every week are taking their own lives in the North each year. It also reported that deprived areas in the six counties suffered from suicide rates three times higher than the least deprived areas.

Alarmingly *The Detail* reported that there had been a total of 7,697 suicides (5,666 were males) from the beginning of 1970 to the end of 2015. This is more than twice the number of citizens killed during the decades of war.

Twelve years ago I was the MP for west Belfast, which had – along with north Belfast – the highest suicide rate in the North. In October 2004 I led a delegation of Sinn Féin and community activists to meet with the British direct rule minister, Angela Smith. Families bereaved by suicide were leaders in this endeavour and among the proposals we tabled was the creation of a regional suicide prevention strategy and an all-Ireland strategy. A series of meetings followed with the Department of Health, the Children's Commissioner in the North, and with the North and West Health & Social Services Trust. Protests were also held, and on one occasion I wrote to Mary Harney, the then Minister for Health, requesting a meeting to discuss a suicide prevention strategy for the island. I'm still waiting for a response to that letter.

The intensive lobby in the North succeeded in 2006 in se-curing the establishment of the 'Protect Life' suicide prevention strategy and action plan. Since then over £50 million has been spent on suicide prevention. Undoubtedly many lives have been saved but the recent statistics are evidence that much more needs to be done.

Suicide is also a major issue in the South. In June the Mental Health Commission published its annual report. The state's mental health policy, *A Vision for Change*, has been in place since 2006 and the Mental Health Commission undertook a strategic review as part of developing a new strategic plan for 2016–18. The commission's report illustrates how much remains to be done, including a need for independent monitoring of the *Vision for Change* policy, which is now ten years old.

There are also significant issues around the lack of funding. The current level of funding for mental health is still less than the 8.24 per cent target mental health budget promised in the government's *A Vision for Change* policy document in 2006. The current numbers of staff are about 75 per cent of the recommended number.

According to the Mental Health Commission's report, there is a serious deficiency in the development and provision of recovery-oriented mental health services. This concept, which is about aiding a person's recovery rather than managing the illness, is crucial. The report also states that the reason for this is the combined effect of poor manpower planning, lack of change in professional training schemes, cuts in public expenditure, delays in recruitment and a shortage of appropriately trained staff.

The most recent statistics available for suicide in the South claim that 459 persons – 368 males and 91 females – took their own lives in 2014.

In the North a new 'Protect Life 2' consultation strategy was published this month. It is expected that final publication of the strategy will be in 2017. To be successful it needs to reflect the experience of those bereaved families and community and voluntary groups campaigning on suicide. It also needs to be properly resourced.

Twelve years after the commencement of the campaign for a suicide prevention strategy for the North and over ten years after *A Vision for Change*, the need for an all-island suicide prevention strategy is greater than ever. Such a strategy needs to be properly funded and coordinated and bring together all of the statutory agencies, including health and education. Voluntary and community groups cannot provide this. Governments must do so.

THE
BREAKING BALL

The Long Road to Clones

29 June 2009

Aaaaaaahhhhhhhh! What joy! What sheer unadulterated totally wonderful bloody joy! What a game! What a team! What a victory. I saw the game – Antrim versus Cavan in the 2009 Ulster Football Championship semi-final – in the Fiddler's Green pub in San Francisco just before our big Unite Ireland Forum. Me and Maírtín Óg and RG. At 11 a.m. in the morning. We were joined by Paul and Seamus from Tir Eoghain. They comported themselves with the grace of princely Gaels. All-Ireland champions. And they didn't mind who knew it.

Seamus is a good-hearted young man from Coalisland and Paul is a much older dude from the same parish. Paul told us maybe we would be better going somewhere else for coffee instead of wasting our time thinking we could beat Cavan. I told him we had our sights on Croke Park in September. Seamus laughed.

I told him the old joke about the Tyrone star forward Peter Canavan. You know the one? From the era before Tyrone were the champions? When they were like Antrim!

'What's the difference between Peter Canavan and a Falls Road black taxi?

'A black taxi can only carry six passengers.'

Seamus stopped laughing.

'I see your point,' said Paul.

'You'll see lots more points in the next seventy minutes,' I shot back at him.

We can win, I told myself. This time we can win. Other times in the football, we drew the big hitters in Ulster but Cavan was

245

doable. All winners need a wee bit of luck sometimes; ours was the luck of the draw. I could hardly dare to believe it. But I did. We could win. Antrim could get through to the Ulster final.

There were two Cavan people at the table behind us. A man and his young son. A couple from Kerry and some Galway folk sat on high stools at the bar. Me and the Cavan duo wished each other luck. Then the game started.

I can't remember the exact details of it; I'd need to see it again. A hundred times over. We started slowly, as I recall. Cavan were more assertive. They had more possession. But their first effort at a score was a wide. That looked promising. Then another few wides and I felt that things could turn out okay. My confidence grew, even though we were on the defensive.

Then we started to exert ourselves. The rest is a blur. I remember screaming a lot. And shouting advice at the Antrim lads – Terry O'Neill, Tomás McCann, Niall McKeever, James Loughrey, Justin Crozier, our Gearóid and Kevin Brady.

At half time Maírtín Óg ordered a fry: bacon, sausages, black and white pudding, three eggs, soda and potato bread. I ate half of it as Paddy Cunningham stroked over a point or two. Seamus ordered a fry as well. I ate most of that also as Cavan came back at us in the second half. He didn't seem to mind. I could see he was impressed by the Antrim backs. I was lucky we weren't drinking. A Coalisland man and his drink would not be so easily parted.

'We need to watch out for the soft goal. A sneaky goal wud have us in trouble,' I announced to no one in particular but in the hope that the Aontroim defenders were listening.

Paul agreed.

'Five points is nothing in football.'

I could have done without that observation, true and all as it might be.

How many times were we here before? Ahead. Playing like

demons. Then our focus goes, our coherency disappears, we stutter and stop playing as a team. We get overwhelmed. We lose.

'Up Antrim,' I screamed. 'C'mon lads. *Aontroim abú.* Up Antrim! Youse can f***ing do it.'

Seamus looked at me disapprovingly. Then Cavan scored the goal.

The Cavan duo behind us applauded like men gone mad.

I never flinched. I was back in the Falls Park playing for Saint Finian's against Saint Gall's. I was nine. Saint Gall's had just scored a goal. I was left half-back. Seán Loughran's quick kick out found me. I went off on a long penetrating solo run before sending a perfect soaring ball forward. Failey Magee fielded it magnificently. He got a point, the winning point. The next day, in the back row of Brother Christopher's class, Seán Loughran and I discussed how we would win two All-Irelands for Antrim. For hurling as well as football.

So Cavan's goal didn't rattle me. But I had fifty-one years of almost being an All Star to reassure me. Minnie Mo, who had been texting me every five minutes from Clones, broke. She couldn't watch the rest. And all the while Saint Finian's Under Tens were alive and well and running at the Cavan defenders like deer. And then Paddy Cunningham gave us another point.

Two minutes into injury time and all Cavan needed was another goal. But I never gave up hope. My heart stopped a few times but the sight of our team playing like dervishes revived me – at least seven times. And then the ref blew it up.

AAAAAAHHHHHHHHHHH!

I phoned our Gearóid at Clones on the mobile. He was jubilant. I was crying.

'Youse have no chance against us,' Tyrone man Seamus declared as we left the Fiddler's Green.

But I could see he was shook.

'See you in Clones, Seamus,' I said.

'Once every thirty-nine years isn't bad,' he retorted.

'There was a war in between,' I reminded him.

'You can't fight a war and play football,' Richard cut in.

And he should know.

'Remember the black taxi,' I said. 'I love Tír Eoghain but …'

'I know,' said Paul. 'It's all on the day.'

Paul is right. Which is strange in itself. But I have to agree.

As David told Goliath, anything can happen on the day.

Aontroim – Ulster hurling champions.

Aontroim – Ulster football champions?

See you in Clones.

The Poc Fada
and the Stormont Estate

19 July 2010

The legend goes that Setanta as a young boy wanted more than anything else to become a warrior and join the Red Branch Knights of Ulster. These were renowned warriors who defended Ireland. Their leader was Conor Mac Nessa, the High King. When he was ten, Setanta told his anxious parents that he was going off to Eamhain Macha (near Armagh) to join the Red Branch Knights. They tried to dissuade him but he was determined. And one sunny morning in May he headed off with his sliothar (ball) and his camán (hurling stick). As he made his way across the Cooley Mountains he would strike his sliothar with his camán and then chase after it, catching it before it hit the ground.

Eventually he reached Eamhain Macha. He joined in a game of hurling with the king's son and others much older than himself and impressed everyone with his skill. Later, he slayed the hound of Culann, the king's blacksmith, by hitting his sliothar down its throat as it attacked him and as a result earned himself the name by which he is best remembered – Cúchulainn – the Hound of Culann.

Fifty years ago a Catholic priest, Pól Mac Sheáin, and the Naomh Moninne club in the Cooley mountains in Co. Louth used this story as the basis for the first Poc Fada (long puck) competition. The purpose was simple – to test the mettle of hurlers by mapping out a set distance in which hurlers hit their sliothar as hard and as far as they could. The winner was the person who covered the course in the least number of pucks.

Some years ago I persuaded Féile an Phobail to hold the west Belfast equivalent of the Poc Fada. It is very popular and Rossa GAC has run it every year since. It has been held in GAA grounds, the Falls Park and on the Black Mountain above the city. It's great craic and all of the participants enjoy the camaraderie and competition.

In November 2009 I hosted a tree dedication ceremony in the grounds of the Stormont estate to mark 125 years of An Cumann Lúthchleas Gael (the GAA). That event was to celebrate the positive impact the GAA has had on society in Ireland. In the course of it I pointed across to the statue of Edward Carson, who is identified with militant unionism, but who as a student at Trinity College in Dublin was a member of their hurling team. In Montgomery Hyde's biography of Carson, it is recorded that 'on one occasion he was mentioned by a local sporting journal, *The Irish Sportsman*, as having distinguished himself on the field'.

So, when the management of Féile an Phobail (west Belfast festival) came to discuss the 2010 programme for Féile and the arrangements for the Poc Fada, I suggested that I would host the Poc Fada in the grounds of the Stormont estate. Hence the establishment of Poc ar an Chnoc – the Puck on the Hill. And from that came the idea of a celebrity Poc Fada and trophy to commemorate the fact that Carson was a hurler. At the time of writing Marty Morrissey of RTÉ, heavyweight boxer Martin Rogan, Mark Sidebottom from the BBC and Independent TD Mattie McGrath have all signed up to take part.

So 7 August 2010 will see a full day of events on the grounds of the Stormont estate. It will be a day in which young and old, All Stars and first timers, can exhibit their sporting prowess. As well as the Carson competition and trophy, the Poc Fada will include senior men and women's competitions and an under-ten camogie and hurling Blitz which will be held on the top lawn in front of Parliament Buildings.

What money is raised will be given to the 'City of the Angels Foundation' run by Fr Pat Clarke, originally from Co. Clare. A month ago he visited Parliament Buildings and we talked for an hour about his work. The foundation does amazing work in very difficult and dangerous conditions. It comprises a Centre for Art and Culture in a major shanty town (favela) in the Brazilian city of São Paulo, as well as a Centre for Art, Ecology and Spirituality situated in the Atlantic forest, two hours from the city. Through the medium of the arts, the foundation tries to prevent children of the shanty towns from falling victim to drug culture, to violence and to organised crime.[1]

Finally, a word of thanks to all of those who have helped make this possible: Máire Grogan, Paula McManus, Catherine Murphy, Pat Maginn, Niall Maginn, Gerry McClory, Seán McGuinness, Denis Rocks, Mary Herald and Bridgeen Heenan, and Martin Donnelly from M. Donnelly & Co. Ltd, Dublin.

---

1   Anyone looking for more information on the City of Angels foundation or the work of Fr Pat Clarke and his colleagues should check out www. sitiodosanjos.net.br and www.centroculturalvilaprudente.org.br.

Hurling Forever

18 August 2010

I believe that hurling is one of the best things in life. Of that, there can be no doubt. Ever since Gerry Begley and Paddy Elliot introduced me to a hurling stick when I was about five years old, while they were young gladiators representing Dwyer's GAC, the passion for hurling has never left me.

The Christian brothers from Saint Finian's Primary School on the Falls Road, Munster-born to a man, brought discipline and organisation to our juvenile sporting endeavours. There was Brother Benignus, elderly already by my time and nicknamed 'The Bore' because of the mantra-like instruction he shouted from the sideline, 'bore in, bore in'. Brothers Andrew, Christopher and Aloysius were our main mentors, however, and Saint Gall's were our main rivals.

In the back of our class I idled away the time by fantasising about how I would play for Antrim. I never did. Now I idle away the time imagining how good I used to be. The older you get the better you seem to have been – this appears to be a common tendency for sports people in my peer group, spoofers all including mé féin.

My biggest claim to fame was playing for my school, Saint Mary's, on a team captained by Aidan Hamill, the Antrim and Rossa stalwart. My best schoolboy memory was being singled out for praise by our bainisteoir for my performance in a Belfast versus Dublin schools game in Casement Park. I was injured during that game and I limped back and forth between my granny's and school for ages afterwards, wearing my wound like a badge of honour.

Politics intruded into my life not long afterwards. I was a Saint Gall's club man for a wee while until Brother Leopold – nicknamed the Walking Lamp Post – expelled me wrongly for horseplay in the club room. I was innocent of that charge. When he apologised some weeks later I was too young and churlish to go back. Eire Óg became my club. Then O'Connells, but it was all very secondary now to political campaigning and housing agitation and civil rights work.

My Uncle Paddy, a Sarsfield's man, and Francie, a Davitt's stalwart, were handy hurlers. So was my Uncle Dominic. My older brother Paddy was a handy hurler too, as was Paddy Smith. In the days before internment, in August 1971, I remember a squad of us, including young women from the Seán Treacy's club, pucking a sliothar back and forth on the old pitch at McCrory Park. A few years later, in the cages of Long Kesh, when we were refused permission to have hurling sticks sent into us we made our own. Or at least Cleaky and Big Duice and the more practically minded Gaels in our ranks did so by removing lengths of timber from the innards of our Nissen huts and shaping out hurls for the rest of us.

The screws were mightily alarmed and impressed when the Cage Eleven hurlers showed off our skills on the playing fields of Long Kesh. Unfortunately, our boxwood hurleys were no substitute for the real McCoy. Ash is your only man. Cleaky's camáns barely lasted ten minutes. But as he said later, we made our point.

Antrim's senior hurlers and camogs made their point also this year on the national stage. Mighty stuff. They did us proud. So did Naomh Gall club. And juvenile hurling is on the up across the county. Over 200 young Gaels – boys and girls – showed off their skills on the lawns of Stormont just a week or so ago at the Puck on the Hill. Well done to everyone involved: mentors, parents and players. They are out there on pitches across the land on Saturday and Sunday mornings, pulling and pucking and learning stick work and getting good at the best game in the world, and there are great people fostering hurling, some for generations, in clubs across Belfast and Antrim. Well done to them all.

Did any of you watch the Galway–Tipperary game recently? What a match! Have you seen the Cats in action? Did you see Waterford and Tipperary? Will you be in Croke Park for the hurling final? I will. Attending the All-Ireland hurling final is one of the great privileges of my life. The All-Ireland final. Will it be five in a row for Kilkenny? Or will Tipp win the day? The Cats are favourites, but nobody knows. That's the thing about it. It's all on the day. And what a day it will be.

And another thing about it. The youngster you see with the hurl in his or her hand making their way up the Falls Road or in Dunloy or the Glens could go on to wear our county's colours in Croke Park. They could score the winning point that brings the Liam MacCarthy cup to Antrim. So encourage them. It's all to play for.

THE IRISH LANGUAGE

Culture and Language
in Twenty-First-Century Belfast –
a Catalyst for Change

14 May 2010

The second biannual Gaeltacht Quarter Conference took place in Coláiste Feirste on 14 May 2010. Entitled the Destiny Decade – *Deichniúr an Chinniúna* – it had four broad themes: to look at the challenges and opportunities of community development; to examine how local areas can develop strategies to attract business; to look at how education infrastructure planning can help local areas; and to examine how regeneration can contribute to good relations.

The twenty-first century will see significant changes to the population and infrastructure of Ireland as we seek to compete in an ever more competitive global market. A recent report – 'Infra-structure for an Island Population of Eight Million' – by the Irish Academy of Engineering in partnership with InterTradeIreland, has mapped out some of the likely changes. The report predicts that within twenty years this island will have a population of eight million, with four million people living along the Belfast–Dublin corridor. It believes that with the appropriate infrastructure and investment this corridor can compete with other major European urban zones. And it argues for major infrastructure investment in the growth city regions of Ireland, including Belfast.

Leaving aside the ongoing political movement towards the end of the union with Britain and towards the reunification of the Irish people, the outworking of this report argues for greater and closer economic co-operation and harmonisation on this island. It entails as part of this transition, in the short to medium term, the movement of fiscal powers and the management of the North's economy away from London and back to Belfast.

As the political institutions evolve and strengthen and deliver, and as the all-Ireland elements deepen, our language and culture will play an increasingly important role in building the economy, ending inequality and bringing people together.

The opportunities are amazing. The challenges will also be formidable. But the Irish language community in Belfast has met and overcome challenges before. So, I am very hopeful for the future.

In partnership with business, and with the voluntary and community sector and with the two governments, I believe the resurgence in our language and culture, and the strategic management of its potential, can make a significant contribution towards making Belfast a better and more prosperous place.

Much has happened over recent years. The decades of conflict, which dominated the latter part of the twentieth century, have ended. The peace process is transforming Belfast. There is a power-sharing Executive and Assembly, all-Ireland institutions, including Foras na Gaeilge, and a political stability that would have been unthinkable only a few short years ago. However, if the promise of change and progress is to be realised, then the structured political and religious discrimination and inequalities that remain deeply embedded in society here must be ended.

That must include an end to the institutional and political opposition that exists to the Irish language and culture. An Ceathrú Gaeltachta – the Gaeltacht Quarter of west Belfast – will meet its ambitious goal of becoming a vibrant cultural quarter. It will develop the services, institutions and resources required for such a goal. But this will be resisted from certain quarters. Strategies and partnerships and alliances are needed to overcome this resistance. This work can be assisted in a logical and rational way by drawing on the abundance of evidence that proves that language and culture and the arts can be key drivers in the process of regeneration and the building of sustainable communities. Our language and culture is tied up in our place names and townlands, in our music and poetry.

The history of the Irish language and culture in Belfast is a proud history. It is a rich history that embraces many from the Protestant but particularly the Presbyterian community.

People like Robert Mac Adam and others who protected and sustained the Irish language, poetry, music and dance through very difficult years of persecution. They understood the importance of the language and culture. They ran Irish language classes, published books and collected oral history and music. We can be sure that they would be delighted at the current revival in the Irish language and culture.

There is now a thriving, vibrant activist community in this city. Thousands of our children have and are passing through Irish-medium education. They enter education at the age of three and many have spent their entire pre-primary, primary and post-primary education learning through the medium of the Irish language. Much of the credit for this can be traced to the Gaeltacht on the Shaws Road – a group of Irish-speaking families who pioneered the promotion of the Irish language in Belfast – and the quiet determination of those who ran the Ard Scoil and An Cumann Chluain Árd, two Irish language centres.

The conflict also brought many people to the Irish language, especially the thousands of political prisoners who learned Irish while incarcerated. They brought the language back into their communities and played a pivotal role in creating a new future for the language and culture in the North. An Ceathrú Gaeltachta is the twenty-first-century manifestation of this remarkable growth in the Irish language and culture. There will be a Ceathrú Gaeltachta because there is a growing community of citizens who wish to live their lives through Irish. That is our right.

The regeneration of Belfast has to take that into account. The reshaping of our society, in whatever form it takes, must help change the patterns of inequality that exist in our society. So, the development of An Ceathrú Gaeltachta provides both a route towards equality as well as a tool for regeneration. At the core of An Ceathrú Gaeltachta is Coláiste Feirste, the fastest-growing Irish-medium post-primary school in Ireland.

An Cultúrlann Mac Adam Ó Fiaich on the Falls Road is also a vibrant centre of culture. It was originally a Presbyterian Church and, on one occasion, a carpet showroom. But in the 1980s it became a meanscoil – secondary school – for Irish-speaking young people. Now it is a successful Irish language centre with its own radio station, art gallery, offices, restaurant, bookshop and theatre.

Close by is St Mary's University which also has an energetic Irish language section. And all around are local businesses and communities, eager to promote the Irish language and grasp its regenerative and business potential.

For many reasons, global as well as local, we need a new economy. This should include a greater focus on culture-based projects designed to generate new employment and revenue and create a climate of regeneration for disadvantaged areas. The growth of language and culture-based projects and districts in cities will act as an economic drawing power which can transform areas. A vibrant cultural quarter can also make a neighbourhood a more desirable place to live and work as successful culture-based projects always attract people and business.

Belfast now has more visitors than ever before. So, my friends,

An Ceathrú Gaeltachta is much more than a quarter for Gaels, though that in itself will be a very fine thing. The development of our language is a catalyst for change, for regeneration, for business, as well as the enrichment and the improvement of the quality of all our lives in this city and on our island.

It is a win-win situation.

Building Gaeilge
for Future Generations

13 September 2016

The Irish language was almost destroyed as a result of centuries of British colonial policy. As arguably the greatest imperial power in human history, successive British governments understood the importance of destroying the native language, identity and culture of a subjugated people to make it easier to control, occupy and exploit them.

Irish history is full of examples of policies intended to deter the use of the Irish language while promoting English. But it is also full of courageous men and women, from all classes and all sections of society, who strove to defend the language and music and culture of Ireland. Here in Belfast one of the most important of these was Robert Mac Adam, a Presbyterian industrialist in the nineteenth century – after whom An Cultúrlann is named – and his family. His uncle, also Robert, had helped found the Irish Harp Society in 1808 to provide a means by which blind boys and girls could learn the harp and thus earn a living. The society also promoted the study of Irish. Robert travelled widely and collected manuscripts in Irish, which he then copied and preserved and which can be seen today in Belfast Central Library and in Queen's University.

And there are others too numerous to name who helped preserve the Irish language and culture, including those who in 1969 established the Gaeltacht on the Shaws Road or the Ard Scoil in Divis Street or An Cumann Chluain Árd in Lower

Springfield, all of which were important centres for the Irish language through the 1940s, 1950s and 1960s. The Ard Scoil was destroyed in a fire in 1984 but An Cumann Chluain Árd is still going strong.

It is no accident that the Irish language witnessed a revival in Belfast and other parts of the North during the years of conflict. While many of us had received some basic teaching in school, especially from the Christian Brothers, and some had gone to the Donegal Gaeltacht in the 1960s, the language was very much a minority interest. But in the course of the 1970s, 1980s and 1990s an estimated 20,000 men, boys, women and girls from nationalist areas went through Britain's penal system. In the cages and H-Blocks of Long Kesh and in Armagh women's prison, and in other jails on this island and in England, political prisoners of an older generation or Irish language speakers from Gaeltacht areas used the time to teach the language to those who didn't have it.

Along with existing Gaeilgeoirí, who loved the language for its own sake and worked valiantly to use and promote it, this new cadre of Irish language speakers joined the efforts to grow the language. Instinctively they wanted their own children to have the opportunity to learn and speak Irish in ways they hadn't. This saw an increase in the demand for Irish-medium education in the North. There is now a thriving, vibrant activist community in Belfast and other parts of the island. Currently, 5,000 children are being taught through Irish-medium education in the North. They enter education at the age of three and many are able to spend their entire pre-primary, primary and post-primary education in Irish medium.

In September 2011 the then Culture Minister Carál Ní Chuilín MLA launched the Líofa Initiative – the word Líofa means 'fluent'. Its objective was to get 1,000 people to sign up to Líofa and commit to improving and using Irish. The target was then revised to 20,000 pledges by 2020. It currently stands at 18,257.

I recently attended the opening of Gacl Ionad Mhic Gioll on the Whiterock Road in Belfast. It is an amazing project and part of a pioneering type of bottom-up community and youth work through the medium of Irish, which is being spearheaded by Glór na Móna, an Irish language youth and community organisation. Gael Ionad Mhic Gioll is a £400,000 capital development project that was jointly funded by An Ciste Infheistíochta Gaeilge, the Department of Culture, Arts and Learning under former Minister Carál Ní Chuilín, and Belfast City Council. An Ciste Infheistíochta Gaeilge was established to distribute eight million pounds in funding secured in 2010 during the political negotiations at Hillsborough Castle. Its aim is to sustain and assist the social, economic and cultural needs of the Irish language communities in the North and assist in the stimulation of economic development.

I commend all of those involved in the project and especially my party colleagues in the Executive, the Assembly and Belfast City Council, including the local Upper Springfield Sinn Féin representatives, who worked in partnership with the local community to secure the land and funding for this project.

The centre is purpose built and includes modern facilities for Irish language classes for the local community, as well as youth facilities. It will enable the Irish-speaking community in the Upper Springfield area to sustain and enhance a whole range of community services and to promote 'Gaelsaolaíocht' – the Gaelic way of life – within the area.

This centre is named after Seán Mackle, who played a significant role in sustaining and developing the Irish language. As an architect and community activist he was intimately involved in the life of west Belfast, including the building of the Shaw's

Road Gaeltacht, the founding of Whiterock Enterprises on the Springfield Road, the reconstruction of Bombay Street after the pogroms of August 1969, and the Ballymurphy Community Centre which is now the site of the nearby Fold apartments.

Seán Mackle was a very practical activist. He told me once that we needed to replace names of buildings and projects with Irish names so that people would use the names. He cited An Cumann Chluain Árd and the old Ard Scoil as examples of this. He said Sinn Féin should have done that with Connolly House and of course he's right. An Cultúrlann is a good example of Seán's philosophy as is Féile an Phobail. It is an honour for Seán and his family to have Gael Ionad Mhic Gioll named after him. But it is also an honour for the Ionad to use his name.

It is of course important to remember that there is still opposition to the language, most obviously to the introduction of Acht na Gaeilge and the resourcing of Irish-medium education. I also have very real concerns about the decisions of DUP Education Minister Peter Weir in respect of Irish-medium education. Specifically, there is the failure by the British government to honour its 2006 commitment in the St Andrew's Agreement to legislate for an Acht na Gaeilge – an Irish Language Act that would ensure that Irish language speakers enjoy equality in northern society. It is my view that the general public is ahead of those unionist politicians who remain opposed to an Irish Language Act and the implementation of a language strategy. There is pioneering work being done within unionist communities by people like Linda Ervine and others who have embraced the language, quite rightly, as their language. They are very much in the tradition of those Presbyterians like Robert Mac Adam who helped save the language in times gone by.

While the struggle to attain full Irish language rights for all citizens has to continue, it is a fact that due to the diligence, vision and hard work of Gaeilgeoirí, huge progress has been made. But that progress has to continue. That is how the Irish language movement has been built and it's our duty to continue to support this work. As Seán Mackle told us at the opening of Gael Ionad Mhic Gioll: 'This is only the beginning.'

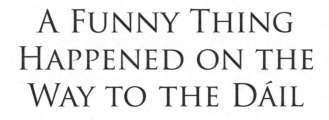

A Funny Thing Happened on the Way to the Dáil

Home Tangus and Don't
Spare the Horses

2 May 2009

So I went off to the west this week. I charged down from Beal Feirste to Galway. Went from there to Maigh Eó and on to Sligo. And then I travelled back to the east coast again, to Dublin.

Being an all-Ireland party is hard work, but at least those of us who are part of all this get to see places that ordinary decent travellers can't reach. And there is always a bit of craic along the way. Take Ballinasloe in Co. Galway, for example. I happened to remark to Tangus, our noble driver, debater extraordinaire and occasional wit, that Ballinasloe hosts the oldest horse fair on the continent. He disputed this. Tangus is like that. Argumentative.

As befits my station, I try to stay above all this. RG, however, who is normally a placid man of few words, is liable – despite my best efforts – to rise to some of Tangus' more provocative assertions. Or denials. So on occasion I have had to intervene when exchanges between Tangus and RG have become overheated. But on this occasion it was I who fell foul of Tangus' caustic tongue.

'Your bum's a plum. How cud the oldest horse fair in the universe be held here?'

We were on the edge of the town, which was an achievement on its own given Tangus' quaint navigating practices.

'I didn't say the universe. I said the continent.'

'Same difference. You are exaggerating. As usual.'

'No, he is not,' RG said. 'Well, not this time, anyway.'

'I don't exaggerate …' I protested.

But RG was in full flow. Reading from Google on his phone, he said, 'The horse fair in Ballinasloe used to be a cattle fair and a sheep fair. *The London Times* refers to it in 1801 ...'

'Brit propaganda,' Tangus cut across him. 'This is a one-horse town if ever I saw one.'

'Don't say that to any of the locals. You'll be hung,' RG warned.

'Hanged,' I said as we clambered from the car to be greeted by Padraig MacLochainn and local councillor Dermot Connolly.

'Fáilte romhaibh,' said Dermot, 'welcome to Ballinasloe, the venue for Europe's largest horse fair.'

'Youse have him primed to wind me up,' Tangus accused me. 'Yis think I came up the Lagan in a bubble.'

Padraig eyed him suspiciously. I could see he was displeased. It takes a lot to displease Padraig, with his enthusiasm, knowledge and good humour. He listened as Tangus challenged Dermot. RG winced.

'I suppose you have a few ponies yourself,' Tangus queried.

'Indeed and I do. Too many,' Dermot responded pleasantly. 'Wud you like to buy a nice Connemara pony?'

'Napoleon's favourite charger was bought here,' Padraig informed us.

Tangus laughed loudly.

Padraig eyed him up and down. Padraig knows his horses. 'Yes, here at Ballinasloe. Its name was Marengo. He was bred in Kilmuckridge in Wexford. Napoleon rode him at Waterloo.'

'Aye,' exclaimed Tangus, 'and Roy Rodgers got Trigger here.'

'No,' says RG, 'you're thinking of the Lone Ranger.'

'Hi ho Silver away,' chortled Tangus.

That's when RG broke. Before any of us could stop him he was frogmarching Tangus back towards our car.

'He says this is a one-horse town,' he shouted by way of explanation at our startled welcoming party.

'What?' chorused Dermot and Padraig.

'String him up,' someone muttered under their breath.

I tried to calm the situation but I was swept to one side as Tangus was wrestled from RG's grasp by the Ballinasloe Shinners and half carried, half dragged towards the town square. By the time I reached there he was perched on top of a large bronze statue of a horse.

'Okay, okay, I'm sorry,' he was telling them. 'This bloody horse is wet,' he continued.

'Serves you right,' RG admonished him.

'Now do you believe that the Ballinasloe horse fair is the biggest in …'

'In the whole wide world,' Tangus agreed.

They let him down after that and we got back to politics and the large-ish crowd that gathered to watch Tangus' show trial. They thought Tangus was a Fianna Fáil minister. They were disappointed but Padraig glad-handed them all with terrific cheerfulness anyway. They seemed impressed.

Later, as we left Ballinasloe, Tangus was silent.

'You know Tangus,' RG told him. 'Napoleon's horse Marengo died of old age in 1832 and his skeleton was kept as a war exhibit by the Brits. One of his hooves is kept at Saint James's Palace in London. After the changing of the guard at Buckingham Palace when the captain is having lunch, Marengo's hoof is set out with all the other regimental silver.'

'The Brits are funny like that,' I said. 'They took Sonny Riley's horse up in the Murph one time …'

'I'm talking about Napoleon, not Sonny Riley,' RG snarled.

'Sonny was a sound man,' I said.

'Straight from the horse's mouth,' said RG.

'Know alls,' Tangus muttered. 'Know alls who know … all.'

We headed for Mayo. Only 200 kilometres to go.

Wet, Wet, Wet

24 August 2009

Almost a year ago, on the cusp of RG's last birthday, a few friends informed him that they had gathered together their meagre monetary resources. They intended to buy him a fitting present as a sign of their great love and affection for his aging personage. RG protested, as one does, saying that there was nothing he wanted or needed. Although deeply moved by their generosity, he told them that he was also mindful of the poverty in which they existed. They had their families and other burdens to carry. Be that as it may, he was told firmly that his *compañeros* had contributed to marking his *lá breithe* and it would be better that it be with something he wanted instead of something for which he would have no use.

Finally they wore him down. Friends can be like that sometimes. Trying. Very trying, as RG observed to me. One particularly long-standing amigo of mine once remarked to me that you didn't have to like your friends to be friends with them. I understand that he didn't contribute to the birthday collection. Maybe he was trying to prove his point? Anyway, RG eventually gave in.

'Wet gear,' he said, 'wet gear would be nice, thank you very much, though you know you don't need to get me anything.'

The birthday arrived bountifully. So did the wet gear. RG had pictured himself whistling cheerfully up Donard or along Sliabh Dubh in the very finest of gortex pants and matching jacket. Would they be revolutionary red? Or a masculine blue? Maybe patriotic green?

I was there as the wrapping was torn eagerly apart and a black rubber balaclava and black rubber boots with individual big toes tumbled out, to be followed closely by a one piece suit of the same material. Not exactly the clothing for brambley paths or heather-clothed boggy slopes.

'Wet gear?' RG muttered as the truth dawned on him. 'This is a bloody wetsuit!'

A really fine and dandy job, but no use for hillwalking. And not exactly suitable for the Falls Baths.

Of course I kept all this to myself.

And the wetsuit kept itself to itself – until last week.

Last week RG stood in a gale force wind on a deserted beach in Fanad in north Donegal. There was not another sinner in sight as he stripped off and proceeded to slip into his slick new outfit. Getting into it was torturous and slow. The wetsuit resisted every inch of the way. It was a pulling and stretching marathon, a wrestling match with an unsympathetic, wily and rubbery opponent. But eventually leg by leg and arm by arm RG wormed his way into its innards. There was sand everywhere.

Eventually he stood up. In reality, he stooped up. He could hardly breathe. A panic attack threatened. His limbs were constricted. The new goggles steamed up. The balaclava put a halt to his hearing. The wind and the sand whipped around his twisted, contorted Quasimodo form. As he lurched towards the broad Atlantic the tide appeared to be going out. And then to compound his difficulties he realised that he had no towel. He slunk back to the car and drove, wetsuited, balaclaved and begoggled, like a thief, back to the house, scundered in case he met anyone he knew en route.

By the time he got back to the beach he realised that he needed a pee. For a second he contemplated doing it in the suit. But he knew he would regret that. His waters would have no point of exit. His midriff regions would be poached. So he jigged from foot to foot as he tried to strip off what was now a second skin. Peeling a live conger eel would be easier, he confided to me, than taking off a wetsuit with maniacal tactile tendencies while dying for a leak. His jig became a jive, then a slow tango along the strand while all the while his bladder beat its own crazy beat until … eventually … relief! Ahhhhhhhh!

By the time he got the wetsuit on again the tide was even further out. But he was not going to be denied his reward. He trudged seawards until at long last he could plunge into deep water. He lasted all of five seconds. The problem was he couldn't move. The suit had him in a full nelson. He could barely flex his arms.

He also knew now why it was called a wetsuit. He was soaking. He got some slight relief by floating on his back. But his y-fronts were wringing wet. He had kept them on. Under the suit. He was wet, wet, wet. And half strangled.

Later, back among the dunes he thought he would die. The re-match was a prolonged duel. Like a grudge match with a drunken but happy octopus. By the end of it he was exhausted. And close to tears.

But at least as he consoled himself later with a drink or two, he did so in the knowledge that he had conquered the wetsuit. It was now only a matter of practice. What a great birthday present. He would be like a dolphin before long.

The next day, as RG and I watched surfers dancing on the waves on a different strand, he told all this to me. Suddenly, mid-sentence, he choked and exclaimed, 'The zips of their suits are down their backs!'

I grinned at him.

'My wetsuit was on back to front! Don't you tell anyone,' he begged me.

'Of course not,' I assured him. 'Of course not.'

Go On – Hug a Tree

4 March 2009

I love trees very much. I grow quite a lot of them. Well, that's an exaggeration. Every autumn I gather up seeds and pot them up. When they get to a decent height, I plant them out or give them away. Trees are a lovely way to mark the death of a friend, or a birthday or as a little token of friendship. I also collect my seeds in some of the places I get to visit. So I have rowan seeds gathered at Chequers, the country house of the British prime minister. I have holly from the grounds around Hillsborough Castle. I have a solitary little redwood from the big redwood forest outside San Francisco. Seeds from the White House didn't take, though the ones from 10 Downing Street are struggling on.

My most successful trees are chestnuts from the Falls Park, rowans from everywhere and oak. Anyone could grow chestnuts. They come originally from Baltic countries where the soil is fairly cold, so they prosper in warmer Irish soil. Oaks grow very slowly but I have three, which are thriving. Ash are also easy to grow and, as all Gaels will know, the camán or hurling stick is made from ash.

Twenty years ago I wrote to Belfast hurling clubs and encouraged the ones with little patches of spare ground to plant stands of ash for their hurls. To my knowledge none of them did. No surprise then that ash is imported, mostly from Eastern Europe, to make the vast majority of hurls in Ireland today.

There are over 100 hurley manufacturers and about 20 commercial producers making between 10,000 and 20,000 hurleys every year. That's a lot of ash. But about one and a half acres of trees can produce about 4,000 sticks. So there you are. Grow your own camán. Plant one now. That would be in keeping with the theme of the 2009 National Tree Week: 'Our Trees – Our Culture'.

In passing, let me congratulate the Antrim hurlers for a magnificent victory over a valiant Wexford side last Sunday, 1 March, in Casement Park (Antrim beat Wexford 4–16 to 4–12). It was a wonderful advertisement for the best game in the world. By the by, Antrim is one of six Irish counties whose name is associated with trees: *Aon Troim* or Elder. This could also be a single ridge or single dwelling. The others are: Derry or *Doire* – oak; Monaghan or *Muineachán* – place of thicket; Kildare or *Cill Dara* – church of the oaks; Mayo or *Maigh Eo* – plain of the yews; and Roscommon or *Ros Comáin* – Saint Comain's Wood. Trees also feature in the names of towns, villages and townlands throughout the island. The most common are oak – Durrow, Coolderry, Derrylin and Edenderry to name a few – and yew – Terenure, Newry, Youghal. Alder incidentally gives us Ferns down in the sunny south-east.

Some trees are sacred and these were known as 'bile'. They feature in names like Rathvilly or Moville.

Only 10 per cent of Ireland is wooded, compared to the EU average of 36 per cent. So we have a lot of planting to do, but plant only native species, as they will encourage native insects, which in turn will encourage native birds, including some like the curlew and the redshank that are under threat. And that's what makes the world go round. Touch wood.

And just in case you didn't know it, that expression comes from the time of the druids when we worshipped trees and warded off evil spirits by touching a piece of wood.

Or why not branch out? Hug a tree. Go on. It will do you good. And the tree will be pleased.

Hair Today – Gone Tomorrow

7 January 2016

Isn't it funny that women are said to get their hair 'done'. Men get their hair 'cut'. I hate getting my hair cut. But I wouldn't mind getting my hair done. The problem is that no matter what you tell them most barbers seem afflicted with a desire to cut as much hair as possible.

When you wear glasses, as I do, you have to remove them for the shearing session. So things are a bit of a blur until the process is concluded and then what can you say? Nothing, except, 'That's grand.'

I've known many barbers. Some of them talk incessantly, about everything – especially politics. I hate that. RG hates that, too. He confided in me one time that as well as being short-sighted, he's becoming slightly deaf. So as well as not seeing what's happening to his head he can't hear what he's being interrogated about. Although I don't think he'll have to worry about the barbers for too long!

The worst barbers I ever met were in Long Kesh. I think some of them did it as a joke. Or as a protest against internment. That's why my hair and beard were shoulder length.

And then there are other barbers who flit in and out of your life. Cutting your hair almost on a whim. These are usually nieces or other female relations who dress hair for a living or as a hobby. Usually they don't charge you.

Anyway, I am drawn to this subject because of a recent experience and because I don't want to write about politics for once. I had managed to avoid getting my hair cut for a long time

– well longer than usual – when I was pulled in by the Sinn Féin style police. Your hair and beard are too long, they told me. Get them cut, I was instructed.

It turns out getting a haircut in Dublin can be a bit of a challenge.

'I wouldn't mind going to a Turkish barber,' I said to RG as we sat gridlocked along the quays in early morning traffic.

'There's one at the corner of Holles Street,' he said. So we meandered our way in that direction.

I told RG about the Tyrone woman's husband going to a Turkish barbers because for every three haircuts you got the fourth one was free. We both agreed that that seemed like a good deal. But when we reached Holles Street the Turkish barbers was closed. Getting parked was another problem.

It wasn't long past 9 a.m.

'I'll drop you off,' said RG. 'It should be opening soon.'

'Where will you go?' I asked.

'I'll drive round,' he replied. 'See you back here in half an hour.'

So that's what we did. I felt a bit conspicuous standing outside the shuttered shop with its posters proclaiming hot towels, shaves and other mysterious procedures. So, I went for a walk.

A homeless man hunkered down in a doorway greeted me cheerfully. He was wrapped in sleeping bags.

'Do you know when the Turkish barbers opens?' I asked him.

'No,' he replied. 'I haven't been to the barbers in years.'

We talked for a few moments about the recession, the Taoiseach and the peace process before I wandered back. Still no sign of the Turkish barber opening. I loitered for another while until RG pulled into the kerb.

'Maybe it's closed,' he suggested.

'Of course it's closed,' I said, more sharply than I intended.

'No, I mean closed-closed. Check it out in that supermarket,' he instructed me. 'I'll do another circuit,' he said, driving off with great patience.

The supermarket wasn't really a supermarket. It was a corner shop. The young woman behind the counter looked as if she was Polish. She was tall and angular and had a nice smile.

'Do you know when the Turkish barbers opens?' I asked her.

'It's closed,' she said.

I thought I noticed her eyes misting over slightly.

'Abdullah has left. He said he couldn't get enough customers,' she said.

I imagined Abdullah being drawn from his empty barber shop to the young Polish woman with the nice smile. I imagined him confiding in her about how difficult things were. They were both exiles. I presumed Abdullah was young. She obviously missed him now.

'Where did he go?' I asked.

'Why do you ask?' she replied, as her smile faded.

'Oh, just wondering,' I stammered. 'Thank you.'

'Have a nice day,' she concluded, smiling once again.

Afterwards as we made our way to Leinster House I told RG about the beautiful Polish shop assistant and her Turkish lover.

'A real Turkish delight,' he said gruffly, his patience finally evaporating.

Later that day I surrendered to another barber's chair. I noticed how white my shorn locks were against the dark cape in which I was draped. Not just white – Persil white. And that was only the beard.

'Could you cut that bit here?' I asked. 'It always grows in a big clump.'

'Someday you'll be glad to have a big clump to complain about,' my tormentor responded.

There was no answer to that.

Boxing Clever

4 August 2016

The recent *rí rá* (uproar) about our boxers at the Olympics in Rio, in which Belfast boxer Michael Conlan was judged by fans to have been robbed of winning a fight, brought back memories to me of my own boxing career. I used to box for a club on the Shankill Road in Belfast. It was around the time Johnny Caldwell won a bronze medal for Ireland at the 1956 summer Olympics in Australia. I was eight years of age and I still remember his homecoming on the back of a lorry down and around Cyprus Street and the other terraced streets of the Falls. He was one of our sporting heroes. It's great to see his statue in the Dunville Park.

Freddie Gilroy from Ardoyne was another Belfast fighter who won a bronze medal at the Melbourne Olympics. Jim McCourt later won bronze at the Tokyo Olympics. If I remember rightly, Jim lived at the bottom of Leeson Street. Or at least he had a little bicycle shop there in the front room of his house. I hope I'm right about that. What is certain is that Jim was rated as one of the best amateur boxers in the world. My achievements were much more modest.

Dominic Begley was a relation of ours. He was a handy boxer. So, at the height of all the pugilistic excitement of the time, Dominic took me the short walk up Conway Street to the Shankill Road. I think the club was in the YMCA, but maybe not. I know it was close to The Eagle Supper Saloon. I didn't last very long, no more than a few months or so. I perfected the little hissing noise that boxers make when they are throwing or receiving punches and I was very good on the punch bag. The bit I never embraced was when I was put into the ring with some other wee buck who seemed to have a homicidal desire to knock my head in. I never quite conquered the ability to not let my opponents hit me. My instinct was to talk to them. That, however, seemed to compel rivals to hit me even harder and more often.

Poor Dominic Begley was distracted. So was I. Time and time again, he would stop the fight.

'Gerard,' he would entreat me, 'hit him back. Stop talking to him. He is only seven. You're nine. Don't keep backing away. Hit him with a left, then a right and then a left again. And stop making that stupid hissing noise.'

So I did my best. My left-right-left combination became more polished and accomplished. So long as the punch bag didn't strike back. Dominic persevered. He used to spar with me when no one else would. Eventually he gave up and returned me to my granny.

'I'm sorry Aunt Maggie but now that he is wearing glasses I don't think the boxing will suit him.'

I was glad and Dominic was kind. My granny seemed to be glad also.

'Well at least no one will be able to pick on him,' she said, thinking I was now an expert boxer.

Little did I know how true that was to be. Almost.

Actually as it turned out no one would be able to pick on my older brother Paddy. Not when Paddy could say, 'Do that again and I'll get our Gerry for you.'

I remember the day it started. A big boy from across our street hit him one day when we were playing a game of Rounders. Our Paddy was small for his age and he started crying. I challenged his assailant. He told me to mouth away off. Before either of us knew it, I hit him. Not just once. No.

All my months sparring with Dominic Begley paid off. I hit the bigger lad with a left, then a right and, as his knees buckled and his nose spouted blood, I finished him off with another left. He was amazed. So was I. And I never hissed once.

My next street fight was also our Paddy's fault. One of the Dunnes stole his kitten. I was sent out to get it back. Again my winning combination had the desired effect. The cat-napper collapsed on Glenalina Road as I caught him with a left, then a right and another left.

Then I made a mistake. I picked up the kitten, turned my back and started to walk back to where our Paddy waited for his pet. That's when I got hit on the back of the head with a half brick from one of the Dunnes. An Ardoyne upper cut.

Later, when I got out of hospital, I was distraught to find out that our Paddy gave his kitten away. For fourteen marleys, a kali sucker and two gobstoppers, he did the Judas on me and handed the kitten over to the brick thrower.

Fliuch! Fliuch! Fliuch!

I don't mind the rain. I never have. Away back in the day when I was on the run it was easier to wander around west Belfast on a wet day when there weren't a lot of people about and those who ventured out weren't paying much heed to anything except the need to get back indoors again as soon as possible. In the rain you could become invisible. A cap, a parka jacket or a duffle coat hood kept out the drizzle and provided much needed cover from passing British Army jeeps and other trespassers. So the rain and I are good friends.

When I was a schoolboy it wasn't so easy. Not when your shoes were letting in water. My shoes used to let in a lot. It was entirely my own fault. There were no brakes on my bike. So in order to stop or slow down the trick was to wedge your foot in between the front fork of the bike and against the front tyre. This had a debilitating effect on the sole of the brogues. My right shoe had a groove, which eventually became porous. I remember thinking that my Ma was going to kill me when she found out. That was after my friend Joe Magee had the bright idea of making insoles from oil cloth. But that didn't stop the socks from getting soaked. That's the socks which survived. My granny used to darn the lesser damaged ones.

Anyway, once it was discovered how our shoes were getting destroyed it wasn't long before we were forbidden from using our feet as brakes. That was when Joe Magee came up with a wooden wedge as a sort of a brake, which worked, sometimes. That wonderful invention meant that we only had to use our feet in the event of an emergency.

The reason our bikes had no brakes was because Joe Magee and I used to make our own bikes from old frames, bits and pieces of rejected cycle parts and wayward wheels rescued from the dump between Westrock and Beechmount.

For a while we used to collect lemonade bottles up at the Dundrod Road races to finance our perambulatory adventures. In those days you got a few pence for returning empty bottles to the local shop. That was when John Surtees was king of the road. Surtees was a world champion on four wheels and two wheels, winning the world championship four times riding a 500cc motorcycle.

All this was great in the summer when it didn't seem to rain as much as it does these days, so porous footwear wasn't such a big problem, especially with the arrival of plastic sandals. But come the winter and the rainy season the walk back from school was a bit of a squelch. Walking back from school was a frequent occurrence given that the bus fare was usually spent on a bag of broken biscuits from Stinker Greenwood's shop. So it was the young dog for the hard road, skipping the puddles en route and avoiding the overflows along the way.

In time, when I graduated to serious hiking and camping, waterproof boots became *de rigueur*. I also plastered the walking boots with Dubbin wax. Tents were made from a heavy water-proofed canvas. Ground sheets were an optional extra. Joe Magee took himself off sailing in drier, warmer climes and ended up in Australia.

I stayed. I like a soft day.

Then along came modern wet gear. Gore-Tex. Fleeces. Layers. Window wipers on my specs. All this makes it easier.

My Uncle Francie, who came back home from Canada for my mother's funeral in 1992, put it well: 'Ireland would be a great country to live in if we put a roof on it.'

My granny used to say the snow in Canada was dry snow. I couldn't figure it out when she complained about Irish snow being wet.

A friend of mine did a lot of time in prison in France. When he returned home I asked him what the difference was between prison in Ireland and prison in France. He reflected for a long minute before replying, 'Nobody talked about the weather in France.'

Au contraire, we Irish seem to be obsessed by the weather. Little wonder.

I'm sitting here, drying out, scribbling these few words. But I wouldn't have it any other way.

Another friend of mine, a German woman, said one day, 'The Irish weather! A few days of sunshine and you forgive a month of rain.'

That's what I hope for. A chance to forgive the rain before the summer gives way to the autumn.

Ode to a Dog

25 August 2016

Long-suffering readers will know I am a dog lover. That's the way it is. For all my many faults, that may well be one of my redeeming qualities. I was thinking the other day that it may be possible to measure your life by the number of dogs you have known. In my case that would mean I am starting to get old.

My first dog was called Darkie. He was a large black and tan canine that stayed with Granny Adams and me when my Uncles Frank and Seán emigrated to Canada in the 1950s. He was a great dog. I always think of him being big but size is relative. I was only seven or eight at the time, so big then mightn't be so big now.

It's like the schoolyard at St Finian's. When I returned there as an adult it was tiny. But back in the day when Brother Christopher, Mr Nolan, Johnny Blake and Brother Aloysius did their best to educate us, the yard was enormous to wee Falls Road primary school students.

So too with Darkie. In my memory he is about the size of a Wolfhound, or at least as big as a Labrador. When our Abercorn Street North gang used to foray into Getty Street or into the Dunville Park, Darkie was always a great ally against the wee bucks from Getty Street. If he hadn't been with us I'm sure they would have scalped a few of us, or certainly inflicted Chinese water torture on any of us they chanced to capture. Darkie prevented that.

He also never had a dog licence. I have a distinct memory of my Uncle Paddy telling me how he had trained Darkie to walk well behind us if there were any peelers about. Paddy explained to me how he taught the dog to let on it wasn't with us in case we were challenged about its licence. I always thought Darkie was very smart to be able to do that. So was Uncle Paddy for thinking of it.

I don't recall how Darkie died. Or even what age he might have been. My Granny Adams went to Canada for a while and I moved back to the Murph, so I suppose Darkie might have moved in with the Begley's. They lived in Abercorn Street North as well. Funny how important the North bit of that address was to older residents. If any of us said we were from Abercorn Street we usually got corrected. 'It's Abercorn Street NORTH,' we were told.

Funny I've never heard of Abercorn Street South or East or West, though I suppose there may well be such places.

So that was Darkie. He is still alive in my memory – that place of wonderment and imagination. He is the first of a long line of four-legged friends: Rory, Mickey, Shane. Cara 1 and Cara 2. Cindy. Barney. Cocker. Osgur. Nuada, Snowie. Fionn, Fiadh. I hope I haven't left anyone out. All but the last four are in doggie heaven. Nuada is up in the mountains, living the good life. She was too energetic for our back yard, a real hyper hound and handsome too.

Snowie nipped one of the little people in my life. Dogs do that sometimes. Especially wee dogs. She was banished to the MacManus household – the dog not the child – where she now lives a life of ease as befits a madadh (dog) of her disposition.

Fionn is lying at my feet now, snoring gently. He is a gentleman. Biddable. Calm. Patient. He is also a great buddy to the little people in my life and an intrepid fetcher of a well-pucked sliothar – or even a mis-pucked one. He seems to have life sussed out. He is a walking, sleeping, eating four-legged bundle of good-natured doggyness. He also loves me. I love him too, and all his ancestors.

Slán

11 May 2009

Me and Osgur went to the vets last Saturday. Neither of us were too upbeat about that. Osgur is a very old canine. So a visit to the vets is a much more traumatic experience for her than for any other mutt, particularly a young one.

The vets was crowded. A very large wannabe German shepherd, by the name of Lucy, sidled up to us in the waiting room. We knew her name was Lucy because that's what the very nice man she was with called out.

'Here Lucy,' he commanded, 'sit.'

And Lucy sat. She really was very docile. The man she was with explained to me that he was told she was full-bred when he bought her as a pup, but that's not the way she turned out. I told him she was in good order. And she was. He said she was only in to get a booster. I told him Osgur was sick.

'Aye,' he agreed. 'She luks poorly.'

And so she did. I explained to the two wee girls who were also with Lucy that Osgur was very old and between us we counted up her age in human years. It amounted to 105 years of age. The two wee girls were very impressed.

Then there was a bit of a commotion and a woman dashed into the waiting room with a small dog in her arms. They were ushered quickly into the surgery. Her dog was knocked down by a black taxi which didn't stop, we learned later. I advised her owner to report it to the black taxi office. Meanwhile a younger man arrived in with a black Labrador. The Labrador had a white beard not unlike my own. I felt a sense of kinship with him. His name was Paddy. When Lucy came back from getting her booster she attacked Paddy. For a second or two all was chaos until one of the wee girls pulled Lucy away.

Poor old Osgur sat through all this. Then we were called in to see the vet. She looked on very compassionately as I lifted Osgur up onto the table.

'It's amazing she has lived so long,' she said. 'She is very low.'

Osgur looked up at me with her big sad eyes. I stroked the back of her head and between her ears. 'I'm afraid this is the end of the road for her,' I said slowly.

Osgur looked at me unblinkingly.

'It's always a hard decision,' the vet said. 'But once her quality of life goes, it's the best decision for her. Do you want to stay?'

'Yes,' I said.

It was all over in a minute or so. Osgur must have known. Her eyes never left me. I never stopped petting her. When she got the injection she sighed and lay back. Then another bigger sigh and that was that. Poor old Osgur was gone. I gave her a final pat on the head, unbuckled her collar and left.

A New
Ireland

Imagining a New Republic

21 January 2017

The Mansion House in Dublin, which on 21 January 1919 witnessed the first meeting of an independent Irish parliament, was the location for a major conference by Sinn Féin recently entitled 'Imagining a New Republic'. The purpose of the conference was to discuss how this generation of Irish citizens can conclude the unfinished business of 1916 and 1919 and create the conditions for a united Ireland. To succeed it needs political will and thoughtful strategies to win popular support. Political, economic and inclusive arguments which can persuade Irish people – whatever their current political leanings – that a united Ireland is in their self-interest are also required.

It was at that first meeting in 1919 that the First Dáil asserted the national freedom and independence of the Irish people. The vision of the Proclamation, as well as the courage and generosity of the men and women of 1916 – and of those who met in this building three years later – contributed to the production of the Democratic Programme of the First Dáil. It envisaged a republic where people were citizens, not subjects; where they had fundamental rights, not arbitrary privileges; where there was equality, not elitism; and where there was unity, not partition and division. Reflecting the language of the Proclamation, the First Dáil declared 'the right of the people of Ireland to the ownership of Ireland, and to the unfettered control of Irish destinies to be indefeasible'.

Almost 100 years later, the two states created by partition have failed to meet the objectives set by the Proclamation and the Democratic Programme. Partition created two narrow, mean-minded, conservative, elitist, sectarian regimes. In the North, a deeply sectarian unionist regime institutionalised decades of inequality and injustice. In the South, poverty, emigration and inequality were rampant. There was the horror of institutional abuse. Censorship in the arts and culture of this state and its politics was pervasive. Some of our greatest writers were banned. The old, imperial administration was replaced by new, native political and economic elites. They, like the political establishment, believe that our sovereign nation stops at the border.

Partition has had a hugely negative impact on this island. It created a duplication of public and private services, two sets of currencies and two systems of tax, laws and regulations. It also sustained decades of conflict, inequality and sectarianism. The conflict has now thankfully come to an end, but partition and the divisions it has fostered still exist.

Sinn Féin has a vision of a new Ireland in which neither gender nor race, age nor disability, sexual orientation nor class nor creed nor skin colour nor location can be used to deny citizens their full rights and entitlements. We are for a new Ireland, one that builds reconciliation between Orange and Green. A society that is democratic and inclusive, based on equality, freedom and social solidarity, embraces the ethos of the Proclamation and the Democratic Programme, shares its wealth more equitably, looks after its aged and its young, provides full rights for people with disabilities, liberates women and delivers the highest standards of public services.

There are immediate challenges facing those of us who want a united, independent Ireland. These include getting the Irish government to change its policy from one of acquiescing to the union with Britain to one of becoming a persuader for Irish unity, getting the Irish government to begin preparations for Irish unity and engaging with unionism on the type of Ireland we want to create. We need to address the genuine fears and concerns of Ulster unionists in a meaningful way. We need to look at what they mean by their sense of Britishness and be willing to explore and to be open to new concepts.

But what is clear is that partition has failed unionists. It has failed nationalists. It has failed the people of this island. And ending partition has now taken on a new imperative following last summer's Brexit vote. The citizens of England and Wales voted to leave the EU. The people of Scotland and of the North voted to remain. As the dire economic implications of Brexit take shape there is an opportunity to promote a new, agreed Ireland.

The British government's intention to take the North out of the EU, despite the wish of the people there to remain, is a hostile action. Not just because of the implications of a hard economic border on this island but also because of its negative impact on the Good Friday Agreement.

The Good Friday Agreement contains a range of safeguards and legislative measures that are intended to ensure equality of treatment and parity of esteem. The agreement specifically states that the North/South Ministerial Council must consider the EU dimension in all relevant matters, including the implementation of EU policies and programmes, and proposals under consideration in the EU framework. It calls for arrangements to be made to ensure that the views of the council are taken into account and represented appropriately at relevant EU meetings. The agreement also requires that the British government incorporate into the law of the North the European Convention on Human Rights (ECHR). This allows, in the words of the agreement, 'direct access to the courts, and remedies for breach of the Convention, including power for the courts to overrule Assembly legislation on grounds of inconsistency'.

All of that is now at serious risk. The British government has stated its desire to end its relationship with the European Convention on Human Rights. It has also said it intends to scrap the Human Rights Act 1998 which gives legal effect to the European Convention.

The British position also fails to take account of the fact that citizens in the North, under the agreement, have a right to Irish citizenship and therefore EU citizenship.

For our part, Sinn Féin is prepared to work with all parties with a professed united Ireland objective. There is an onus on the Irish government to prepare a real plan for unity. A first step in this would be the development of an all-party group to bring forward a Green Paper for Unity. In addition, plans should be developed for an all-island National Health Service and for all-island public services through a 'United Ireland Investment and Prosperity Plan'.

Now is the time for all parties who support Irish unity to come together to design the pathway to a new, agreed, inclusive united Ireland – an Ireland that is built on equality and which is citizen-centred and inclusive. People in the South need to be convinced that a united Ireland is affordable. People in the six counties need to be convinced that unity will work and that the loss of the British subvention will not impoverish them.

In 2015 economist Michael Burke produced a paper: 'The Economic Case for Irish Unity'. His conclusion at the end of a detailed analysis was that: 'Quite simply put, the whole population of Ireland would benefit economically from reunification.' He added that the two economies on this island 'have clear synergies. These are all significant factors that, if the potential is realised through investment, could substantially raise the prosperity of the whole island.'

And then Professor Kurt Hübner of the University of British Columbia in Vancouver produced his paper: 'Modelling Irish

Unification'. Three unification scenarios were presented, with the most aggressive estimating a €35.6 billion boost in an all-island GDP in the first eight years of unification. It found that there would be long-term improvements in the economy of the North as a result of the removal of currency, trade and tax barriers which currently impede economic growth.

So we now have the opportunity to re-imagine Ireland, an Ireland where conflict and violence are in the past, an Ireland that reflects our genius and diversity, our dignity and our strengths. The Good Friday Agreement and Brexit are changing the relationships within and between the North and South, and with our nearest off-shore island.

The determination of the British government to impose Brexit on the North, despite the vote of the people, underlines the undemocratic nature of partition and the unequal relationship between London and Belfast. The future constitutional position of the North lies in the hands of the people of the North and of the South. Scottish First Minister Nicola Sturgeon, in a recent address to the Seanad, said, 'We are living in unprecedented times and those unprecedented times require imagination, open minds and fresh thinking.'

She is right. It is the time to look to a new future, a different future. Brexit has demonstrated again the failure of partition. Now is the time to look to the future and to talk about, to plan and to deliver a new and united Ireland.

Time for Unity

18 March 2017

The 2016 centenary celebrations of the 1916 Rising were a resounding success. Political, cultural, historical and media organisations, individuals and communities held hugely successful events to celebrate the individuals and the organisations that participated in the Rising. There was lots of music, some excellent exhibitions and interesting debates. The Irish government, which had initially produced a very inadequate and underwhelming programme, went back to the drawing board after ferocious criticism and came up with some very good events. However, official Ireland studiously avoided the issue of partition, its impact on the island and the need for Irish unity.

For Irish republicans this was at the heart of all that we did in Ireland and across the globe to commemorate the Rising, particularly in North America and Britain. The Republic that was envisaged by the leaders of 1916 and by the Proclamation is at the core of our political beliefs. It is the rock upon which our politics and policies are constructed.

Making these policies work requires the building of significant and active support allied to strategies, tactics and programmes of work. In November 2016 Sinn Féin launched 'Towards a United Ireland', a detailed paper setting out the arguments for a united Ireland which addresses the negative impact of partition on the economy, on inward investment, on exports, on the health service, on the border region and much more. It faces head-on the argument that the people of the North and South cannot afford a united Ireland. It takes this on and demolishes it.

What else is new? Fianna Fáil is growing a unity plan; Taoi-seach Enda Kenny is for giving the vote to citizens outside the southern state in presidential elections. The daffodils are bloom-ing and the snow drops as well. Spring is springing. Again. So are Fianna Fáil and Fine Gael. For decades they have wrapped the green flag around themselves when it suited. When the issue of reunification is raised in the Dáil, as it is now regularly by Sinn Féin, the response from the establishment parties is usually that this is not the time to talk about it. Now Irish unity is all the rage in Leinster House.

The decision by the British government to trigger Article 50 to commence the Brexit negotiations, the Assembly election results in March 2016 which saw the unionist parties lose their Assembly majority, and the warning by the Scottish First Minister of a second independence referendum, are the context for discussions on a united Ireland.

The announcement by Micheál Martin that Fianna Fáil is to produce a White Paper on Irish unity is a welcome addition to the conversation that is necessary to inform citizens and assist progress. In 2005 in the Dáil Sinn Féin produced a Green Paper on unity. Following on from the publication of our discussion paper – 'Towards a United Ireland' – last year, and following consultation with many sectors, we have been working on the production of a more advanced version of this paper.

So times are changing and relationships are changing. In his negotiation with the EU over the terms of Brexit, Taoiseach Enda Kenny called for a 'United Ireland' provision to be included in any Brexit agreement. He also announced at the start of 2017 that the government will hold a referendum on Irish citizens in the North and the diaspora having the right to vote in presidential elections. Sinn Féin has been pressing the government on both of these issues. The Taoiseach's announcement was very welcome but the government needs to clarify what it will mean in practice and when the referendum will be held.

After all, the Constitutional Convention voted on this issue in September 2013. A significant majority of its members agreed to extend voting rights to Irish citizens living abroad and in the North. In November 2015 the Joint Oireachtas Committee on European Affairs made a recommendation to extend the voting rights also, following criticism by the European Commission.

In addition, there is also the fact that under the terms of the Good Friday Agreement citizens in the North have the right to Irish citizenship. What will Brexit mean for them and their right to EU citizenship? This is one of the reasons why Sinn Féin believes that the North should have a special status within the EU.

So, that's the battle ahead. To strategise, organise and persuade. There is no shortcut that will work. Sinn Féin's discussion document 'Towards a United Ireland' lays out the rationale for reunification in terms of the benefits to the economy, public services and reconciliation. It also looks beyond the economic benefits of unity. The document details the type of new and united Ireland we believe can be delivered: a new Ireland built on the principles of equality and inclusion; a new Ireland with a new constitution and bill of rights; a new Ireland with symbols and emblems to reflect an inclusive Ireland, that includes the safeguarding of British citizenship and recognition of the unionist identity.

This cannot be a rhetorical debate. There is an onus on the Irish government to plan for unity, to become the persuader for unity. They need to unite with the rest of us for unity, to drive the process and build the maximum agreement and to secure and win a referendum on unity.

A Nation Once Again

There can be a moment in an event that makes the hair on the back of your head stand up, and your throat catch, as emotion threatens to overwhelm you. Just such a moment happened for me on O'Connell Street on the day – 24 April 2016 – that marked exactly one hundred years from the date of the start of the Easter Rising of 1916.

It was a beautiful and crisp Sunday morning. Martin McGuinness and I had joined the crowds at the platform at O'Connell Street outside the GPO. The street was jammed to overflowing with thousands of onlookers. As Martin took to the platform they raised their voices and O'Connell Street echoed to their song.

A Nation once again,
A Nation once again,
And Ireland, long a province be
A Nation once again!

The chorus of 'A Nation Once Again' started as a whisper. Then it grew in volume until the massed choir of thousands of republican voices raised spontaneously in perfect harmony and in tune with the emotion of the morning that was in it. They did the writer of the song, Thomas Osborne Davis, proud.

Davis was one of the founding leaders of the Young Ireland movement in the 1840s and was responsible for some of the best ballads of that period. He published them in *The Nation* newspaper. 'A Nation Once Again' is among his best-known works. It was published in July 1844. It is now part of the Irish tradition.

Sinn Féin had organised the event that Sunday morning to celebrate the exact time the Rising started and to mark Pearse's historic reading of the Proclamation at the front of the GPO. In bright sunshine Dublin City Councillor Mícheál Mac Donncha, dressed as a Volunteer, and Lynn Boylan MEP, dressed in the uniform of Cumann na mBan, introduced the many flags associated with the struggle for freedom. These were accompanied by large posters of each of the leaders of the Rising, including some who died subsequently, like Tomás Ashe who was killed by a force feeding gone wrong during a hunger strike.

Later that day the 'Reclaim the Vision' event took place, which was a citizens' initiative organised by, among others, the artist and activist Robert Ballagh. It was a potent reminder of those transformative days in 1916 when a group of poorly equipped Irish men and women challenged the might of the greatest empire that had ever existed. It was an empire built on conquest, exploitation, brute force and repression.

Following six days of heroic resistance, the centre of Dublin lay in ruins. The leaders of the Provisional Government met for the last time in 16 Moore Street, near the GPO – which was by now in flames – and ordered a surrender. They were court-martialled by the British. Fourteen were executed in the stonebreakers' yard in Kilmainham Gaol. Thomas Kent was executed in Cork. Roger Casement was later hanged in London.

Following their execution Thomas Clarke, Padraig Pearse, Thomas MacDonagh, Edward Daly, Michael O'Hanrahan, John MacBride, William Pearse, Joseph Plunkett, Éamonn Ceannt, Con Colbert, Seán Heuston, Michael Mallin, James Connolly and Seán Mac Diarmada were laid in a quicklime grave at Arbour Hill.

James Connolly was shot to death as he sat tied to a chair.

He faced his court martial with defiance. He was unapologetic, unbowed and unbroken. He said: 'We went out to break the connection between this country and the British Empire, and to establish an Irish Republic.'

An equally defiant Pearse put it best in his address to his court martial on 2 May on the eve of his execution. Imagine the scene: one lone Irish republican facing a court martial of British Army officers. Pearse told them: 'You cannot conquer Ireland. You cannot extinguish the Irish passion for freedom.'

Pearse was not defeated. Connolly was not defeated. The men and women of 1916 were not defeated. But with the execution of the leaders, the main progressive thinkers from the revolutionary period were removed. More conservative elements emerged who accepted the Treaty. A split and bloody civil war followed. This counter-revolution and the partition of the island saw the emergence of two conservative states instead of the thirty-two-county Republic that was the aim of the Rising.

The North became a one-party Orange state where Irish nationalists were excluded from power and denied opportunity. As we all know, that power and privilege was imposed and protected by British guns. Republican resistance was offered at various stages over the decades. In the late 1960s the state's violent response to the democratic demands of the civil rights campaign developed into full-scale armed conflict.

Our country and our people suffered hugely as a result of conflict in the 1970s, 1980s and 1990s. Huge progress has been made in recent years. The peace process and the Good Friday Agreement marked an historic shift in politics on this island. For the first time, the roots of conflict were addressed and a democratic route to Irish unity was opened up. But there is much yet to be done. Wounds must be healed. Divisions ended. The scourge of sectarianism must be tackled and ended.

The effects of partition on the South must also be addressed. By executing the signatories and other leaders the British government prepared the way for partition. They removed the revolutionary leadership and the most advanced and progressive thinkers and activists. They paved the way for the counter-revolution that was to follow the revolutionary period and the establishment of two mean-spirited and narrow-minded states.

During the Civil War the forces of conservatism – the Catholic Church hierarchy, the media and big business – all supported the Free State regime and opposed those who held out for the Republic proclaimed in Easter Week 1916. The Free State was harsh on the poor, on women and on republicans or radicals of any kind. Our native language was devalued and subverted. Most, if not all, of our renowned writers were banned. Censorship was rife. A false morality was imposed on our people.

The scandals we have witnessed recently, particularly the ill-treatment of women and children and the widespread disempowerment of people, emerged from this post-colonial condition. While there have been improvements since it was first established, the southern state is not the Republic proclaimed in 1916. Current efforts by the Dublin establishment to pretend that it is are an insult to the men and women of 1916.

Hardly a week goes by without the emergence of yet another scandal. In a two-tier system, one year after the centenary of the Rising there is still no real accountability and the elites act with impunity.

There are also those who say that honouring the 1916 leaders might retrospectively justify violence. But they say nothing critical of John Redmond and Edward Carson's role in sending tens of thousands of young men, from the Shankill and the Falls and villages throughout the North and the rest of the island, to fight Germans, Austrians and Turks – with whom Ireland had no quarrel –

in the First World War.[1] Over seventeen million people were killed in that imperial adventure. Twenty million more were wounded.

Were John Redmond and Edward Carson not 'men of violence'? Carson was certainly an imperialist – a big house unionist with little concern for the social or economic needs of working-class unionists or the rest of us.

The 1916 Proclamation remains the mission statement for Irish republicans today. Now that the centenary has come and gone there should be more left behind than a memory of a good day out. The time ahead is a time for renewal and planning, for promoting the ideals of democracy and equality.

Our centenary celebrations would have been incomplete without due recognition being paid to the American connection. The Rising was funded by Irish-Americans, who were the children of *An Gorta Mór* (The Great Hunger).

A united Ireland means the unity of the people of this island, including those who see themselves as British. That is why Irish governments must pursue every avenue to promote all-Ireland co-operation and to build relationships between all our people. This must include genuine efforts to reach out to the unionists on the basis of equality.

---

1   John Redmond was the leader of the Irish Parliamentary Party at Westminster from 1900 until his death in 1918. At the commencement of the First World War Redmond urged Irishmen to join the British Army. Tens of thousands were killed or maimed and he was widely criticised. After the Easter Rising of 1916 public sympathy shifted to Sinn Féin. In the 1918 British general election the Irish Parliamentary Party lost 61 of its 67 seats in Westminster.

Edward Carson was a barrister and leader of the Ulster Unionist Party between 1910 and 1921. He campaigned against the 1914 Home Rule Bill, which would have given a measure of limited self-governance to Ireland. In 1912 he was the first to sign the Solemn League and Covenant, which threatened the use of 'all means necessary' to resist Home Rule and he also founded the paramilitary Ulster Volunteers. His leadership of unionism contributed to the partition of Ireland.

There has never been a better time to plan and deliver on an all-Ireland basis. Thoughtful unionists know this makes sense for the economy, agriculture, healthcare, the environment and many other sectors. Elements of the Good Friday and subsequent agreements remain to be implemented.

There is an urgent need for the Irish government to face up to the British government's refusal to fulfil its obligations. There is also an ongoing need to enlist the support for this necessary endeavour of our friends internationally, especially those in the USA, Canada, Europe and in Britain itself.

But the political system and media in the southern state remain deeply conservative and partitionist. Those who oppose political progress and the ideals of the Proclamation remain influential within the political and media establishment.

It is a metaphor of our times that in the centenary year of the 1916 Easter Rising the relatives of the 1916 leaders and their supporters were forced to take the state to the High Court in order to save our national heritage at Moore Street, while the state was defending the interests of a property developer. I commend Colm Ó Mordha and everyone involved in the case.

In 2007 14–17 Moore Street was accepted as a 'National Monument'. This is the place to where, on the Friday evening of Easter Week and with the GPO in flames behind them, the surviving leaders of the 1916 Rising and the men and women of the GPO garrison escaped. Carrying a wounded James Connolly they left the GPO by a side entrance on Henry Street. Under sustained sniper fire from British soldiers they managed to reach Moore Lane and then Moore Street. The garrison entered number 10 and tunnelled from one house to the next until they reached number 16 – Plunkett's – a poultry shop. In a room in this terraced house the members of the Provisional Irish Government held their last council of war. Padraig Pearse, Joseph Plunkett, Tom

Clarke, Seán Mac Diarmada and James Connolly met to decide their next move. It was there that they decided to surrender. This is the 'battlefield site of 1916' but planning permission has been sought for much of it to be concreted over to make way for a shopping mall!

For the last ten years the families of the leaders have fought a protracted legal and political battle to save Moore Street. Last year the state finally agreed to the establishment of the Moore Street Consultative Forum. It comprised Oireachtas representation, Dublin City councillors, 1916 relatives groups, Moore Street campaigning groups, street traders and other relevant stakeholders. Its aim was to consider how best to preserve and present the history and legacy of Moore Street. It published its conclusions in March 2017. The report was widely welcomed. However, the key to the future of this site is ensuring the implementation of its recommendations. I want to commend the families of the 1916 leaders.

It is not a surprise that the proposal for a 1916 banner erected by the Dublin City Council in Dublin's College Green, which didn't feature any of the 1916 leaders, came from the Taoiseach's department. The banner was in line with the government's widely criticised initial video promoting the 1916 celebrations that did not include any reference to the men and women who fought in the Rising. How could that be so?

The Irish government has no intention of bringing about the society envisaged in the Proclamation and supported by the men and women of 1916. It knows the promise and potential of the Proclamation is not reflected in modern Ireland, except in the hearts and needs of the people. It wanted the 1916 centenary to pass as quickly and as unobtrusively as possible.

But during the centenary year, the vast majority of Irish people at home and abroad proudly celebrated the 1916 Rising and the

Proclamation of the Republic. So that is the challenge facing us. To join with others to convert that pride into active support for a real republic.

We must give all our children the best possible chance to fulfil their potential and to live happy, full and contented lives. We love Ireland. We value this small island.

It is the people who are at the centre of our core values of equality, liberty and fraternity. So our resolve must be to end all divisions and to unite our people. Before the Volunteers left the GPO, Padraig Pearse told the women that the fight would not have lasted so long without them and when the history of that week would be written the highest honour and credit should go to the women. So we salute all our sisters in struggle. The Proclamation addressed Irishmen and Irishwomen at a time when women did not have the vote. There can be no *Saoirse na hÉireann gan Saoirse na mBan* – no freedom of Ireland without women's freedom.

The reactionaries and revisionists, the naysayers and begrudgers, the modern-day Redmonites pontificate and waffle about how wrong 1916 was. Sinn Féin has always been crystal clear on this. The attendance at centenary events, the huge number of local commemorations, the pride and popular support for the men and women of the Easter Rising are proof that the vast majority of Irish people believe 1916 was right. The men and women of that Rising were right.

It was Republic against Empire. Republicanism versus Imperialism. We know what side we are on. We stand by and for the Republic.

The 1916 Proclamation is unfinished business. The Irish establishment knows and fears that. It is a freedom charter for all the people of this island that guarantees religious and civil liberty and promotes equal rights and opportunities for all citizens.

The Proclamation is also a declaration of social and economic intent for a rights-based society in which the people are sovereign.

Imagine an Ireland with a public health service and affordable childcare. An Ireland where a home is a right, not a dream.

Imagine an Ireland where your children can return to live, work and to raise your grandchildren. An Ireland where everyone pays their fair share.

Imagine an Ireland where Orange and Green and everyone else is living peacefully together. Where equality rules.

Imagine an Ireland, all thirty-two counties, that is the best place in the world to grow up in, to grow old in, to enjoy life in.

Such an Ireland is possible.

Addendum

In its judgement in June 2016 the High Court found that a greater number of the buildings in Moore Street than those currently recognised by the government should be part of the National Monument. The government decided to appeal this decision. That appeal case has not yet been heard. In March 2017 the report of the Moore Street Consultative Group recommended that the Moore Street historic battlefield site should be preserved in its entirety. An Advisory Oversight Group was set up to implement the recommendations. On 12 July 2017 I raised the government's decision to appeal the High Court judgement with Taoiseach Leo Varadkar during Leader's Questions in the Dáil. I asked him to drop the government's appeal. He refused and confirmed that the government intends continuing with the appeal. The campaign to save Moore Street continues.

POSTSCRIPT

After the Good Friday Agreement was reached in April 1998, Senator George Mitchell remarked to Martin McGuinness and myself that that was the easy bit. The hard bit, he said, would be implementing it – and as the years have shown, he was right. The political process since then has been essentially a continuous process of negotiation, with the occasional crisis thrown in. Yet, despite these stresses, the power-sharing institutions have demonstrated their capacity to work, make local government more accountable and accessible, and change people's lives for the better.

But no one should underestimate the determination of unionism, allied to the political system – the so-called permanent government, which is still mainly unionist at its most senior levels – to oppose change and to maintain their perceived status as top dog, no matter the cost.

I write this postscript on the day after the talks on how to re-start power-sharing at Stormont ended without agreement. These talks were about agreeing the basis for re-forming the Northern Assembly and its Executive, which have not met since January. The collapse of the Executive and of the subsequent elections were triggered on 9 January when Martin McGuinness resigned as Deputy First Minister. In his resignation letter Martin explained that the:

> equality, mutual respect and all-Ireland approaches enshrined in the Good Friday Agreement have never been fully embraced by the DUP. Apart from the negative attitude to nationalism and to the Irish identity and culture, there has been a shameful disrespect towards many other sections of our community. Women, the LGBT community and ethnic minorities have all felt this prejudice. And for those who wish to live their lives through the medium of Irish,

elements in the DUP have exhibited the most crude and crass bigotry.

Speaking to journalists afterwards he said:

> There will be no return to the status quo. The situation we have been dealing with over the course of recent years is unacceptable. I have called a halt to DUP arrogance and if the DUP think in the aftermath of an election that they are going to step back into ministerial positions short of resolving the critical issues I have identified, then they are living in a fools' paradise.

The tipping point for Martin McGuinness was the emergence of the Renewable Heat Incentive (RHI) scandal towards the end of 2016. The RHI, set up by the DUP's Arlene Foster during her time as Minister in the Department of Enterprise, Trade and Investment, aimed to encourage the use by business and individuals of a more environmentally friendly heating method. The more heat a business used, the more money it received and for every £1 spent on fuel, £1.60 was given as a subsidy. However, the scheme was poorly thought out and no cap on subsidies was set. Consequently, it was revealed that the final bill for the taxpayer over the next twenty years would be £400 million.

As a result of Martin's actions an Assembly election was held on 2 March. This election saw the Sinn Féin vote substantially increase. The DUP lost ten seats. The unionist parties also lost their majority status in the Assembly for the first time in a local assembly/parliament since partition, almost 100 years ago. Sinn Féin refused to go back into the power-sharing arrangement with the DUP unless significant changes were made and talks with an eventual deadline of 29 June for agreement were arranged.

But before renewed negotiations could really make progress,

British Prime Minister Theresa May announced a snap general election. This was held on 8 June. When it was over the Tories had lost thirteen seats and their majority. In the North the DUP had succeeded in squeezing out the Ulster Unionist Party in South Antrim, and when Sinn Féin won the Fermanagh–South Tyrone seat from the UUP, that party was left with no Westminster seats. The SDLP lost their three seats – two of them to Sinn Féin. Sinn Féin took seven seats, the largest number ever held by a nationalist party at Westminster. The DUP won ten seats in all. The final seat in the North was taken by independent unionist Sylvia Hermon.

Almost immediately after the election, negotiations recommenced in the North to restore the Assembly. At the same time a separate negotiation involving the DUP and the Tory government also commenced as Theresa May set out to form a minority government. Her objective was to forge an agreement which would see the DUP back the Tories on crucial votes.

On 15 June Michelle O'Neill, the Sinn Féin leader in the North, and I led a delegation from the party to meet Theresa May and Secretary of State for the North James Brokenshire. We warned that doing a deal with the DUP carried huge risks, not least in the threat it could present to the Good Friday Agreement. But, regardless, the deal was struck and in return for DUP support the British government gave an extra one billion pounds for infrastructure and other projects for the North.

For its part the DUP agreed to support the Tory government's austerity policies and further cuts to public services. It also agreed to support the Tory government on all motions of confidence, the Queen's speech, the budget, finance bills, money bills, supply and appropriation legislation and estimates, and all legislation pertaining to British national security and Brexit. This gives the Tories a majority to push through their legislative programme, austerity agenda and Brexit plans.

In addition, the DUP–Tory alliance allows Theresa May to pursue her commitment to scrapping the Human Rights Act, end the jurisdiction of the European Court of Justice in Britain and end the role of the European Convention on Human Rights. If she does so, this would directly contravene the human rights core of the Good Friday Agreement.

The DUP have been emboldened by their new alliance with the Tory Party. The British government has pandered to their anti-rights, anti-equality agenda. This tacit endorsement of the DUP's stance has been driven in large part by Theresa May's desire to stay in power, and to do so she is prepared to tolerate the denial of rights here which are the norm in England, Scotland, Wales and the rest of Ireland. This is not acceptable and cannot be tolerated. I look especially to Taoiseach Leo Varadkar to make this clear to Theresa May. The Irish government has an obligation and a duty to do so. It is a co-equal guarantor with the British government of the Good Friday and other agreements.

It should not be a shock to any informed reader that the DUP comes to the issue of rights slowly and reluctantly. But they cannot ignore these forever. Rights-based policies and agreements are essential for political institutions to be sustainable, especially in the face of Brexit, the London government's austerity policies and the Tory–DUP agreement. The reality is that the Sinn Féin electorate will not consent to be governed by the DUP on their terms, just as we do not and would not expect the DUP electorate to consent to be governed by us on Sinn Féin's terms.

When it comes down to it, getting the Assembly and Executive back on track is quite simple really. It's about rights and it's about equality, things that are good for everyone. It's about agreement on how these are going to be delivered. That's the only way to get the institutions back in place. I have said that very directly to the DUP. I have said the same thing to the British government.

But a step change in the approach of the DUP and the British government is necessary for this to happen.

Will the political institutions be back in place by the time this book is published? I don't know. They should be. But the reality is that a deal has not been done as I pen these lines. This constitutes a monumental failure by Theresa May and her government. Decades of hard work are being put on hold to keep her in power.

Of course, the DUP–Tory deal is a temporary arrangement. I have no doubt that it will end in tears. And when it is over, the issues which the DUP must face up to in Ireland will remain if they have not been dealt with by then.

As the DUP leader, Arlene Foster, reflects on all of this she should be mindful of the words of her predecessor Edward Carson speaking in 1921 on the Tory intrigues that led him on a course that would partition Ireland: 'What a fool I was. I was only a puppet, and so was Ulster, and so was Ireland, in that political game that was to get the Conservative party into power.'

For our part Sinn Féin will continue to prioritise the establishment of a credible, sustainable Executive to deal with all the challenges facing our society, including the failure to implement previous agreements and the consequences of Brexit.

Meanwhile, the Irish government must vigorously pursue the rights of citizens currently being denied by the DUP and the British government. The rest of us must encourage this.

One thing is certain. If we are to build a new Ireland that holds all its citizens equal then we must never give up.

Useful Contacts

A number of sensitive issues are discussed in this book. Below are contact details for organisations that can help you if you are affected by any of these issues.

'Violence against Women: a Cause and Consequence of Women's Inequality'
If you live in the Republic of Ireland:
To contact Women's Aid, freephone: 1800 341 900; telephone: 01 6788858; email: info@womensaid.ie

If you live in Northern Ireland:
To contact the Domestic and Sexual Violence helpline, telephone: 0808 802 1414; Twitter: @WomensAidNI; Facebook: www.facebook.com/WomensAidNI

'An All-Ireland Suicide Strategy is Essential'
If you live in the Republic of Ireland:
To contact the HSE suicide prevention helpline freephone: 1800 222 282

Suicide Down to Zero can be contacted at suicidedownto zero0000@gmail.com

Save Our Sons and Daughters (SOSAD) can be contacted at 041 984 8754 or go to www.sosadireland.ie

To contact Pieta House freephone: 1800 247 247; or simply text HELP to 51444

If you live in Northern Ireland:

Lifeline, the crisis response helpline service for people who are experiencing distress or despair, can be contacted confidentially on 0808 808 8000

Public Initiative for the Prevention of Suicide and Self-Harm (PIPS) is a support service for people who need intervention or for those who have survived suicide loss. Telephone: 086 1933074; or go to www.pipsproject.com

The Samaritans can be contacted island-wide by telephone on 116 123; or email: jo@samaritans.org

ALSO BY GERRY ADAMS

Falls Memories (1982)

The Politics of Irish Freedom (1986)

Free Ireland: Towards A Lasting Peace (1986)

A Pathway to Peace (1988)

Cage Eleven (1990)

Who Fears to Speak …? The Story of Belfast and the 1916 Rising (1991)

The Street and Other Stories (1992)

Selected Writings (1994)

Before the Dawn: An Autobiography (1996)

An Irish Voice: The Quest for Peace (1997)

An Irish Journal (2001)

Hope and History: Making Peace in Ireland (2003)

The New Ireland: A Vision for the Future (2005)

An Irish Eye (2007)

My Little Book of Tweets (2016)

FOLLOW GERRY AT:

www.leargas.blogspot.com

Twitter: @GerryAdamsSF

Facebook: Gerry Adams TD